FEINER

Vielicska

Samuel

Katherine — Regina — Jacob Gross

卐Henrik Engel — Yolonda — Irene

Tomas — Tomas

LOWY

Géza 卐 Abraham — Lena

Endrew — 卐Szeren — 卐Zolton — Helen 卐 — 卐Monci — Gyula 卐 — 卐Michael — 卐Lina

Aranka — 卐Ibi — Anci — 卐Laszlo — 卐Nandor — Irene

Armin

卐? — 卐? — Eva — Marika

REISS

Ignatz

Gissell

'Stephen — Klari

Marianne — Tibor Vayda

Vivian — Ronald — Zsuzsi — Tomas

10634

B
Bal Balshone, Benjamin

Determine

Determined!

DATE DUE

Demco, Inc. 38-293

Determined!

BENJAMIN BALSHONE

Bloch Publishing Company, Inc. New York

—

1 Holocaust. Personal narratives
I Title

Library of Congress Catalogue Number 84–070148

ISBN: 0–8197–0494–6

Printed in the United States of America

ACKNOWLEDGMENTS

To all those people who gave me moral support, encouragement, cooperation, advice, photographs and even of themselves I am grateful. I mention no names for fear of inadvertently omitting someone. You—each one of you—knows the importance of your contribution toward posterity.

Since professionals exist on recommendation, I wish to thank (in alphabetical order) Charles Bloch, Jonathan Cohen, Dr. Hugh Harter, Gertrude Hirschler, Norma J. Lind, Scott Meredith, Dr. Richard Nelson, and Dr. Donald Sanders.

Thanks go to my own office staff for giving of themselves over and above the call of duty; the added chores that were thrust upon them often without warning they executed flawlessly and cheerfully.

I wish to acknowledge the fine cooperation of the staff of Ohio State University for the use of their marvelous library facilities.

Zsa Zsa Gabor referred to Marianne as my "Elet-tars." The Hungarian term (now that I understand its meaning) is totally appropriate. I thank Marianne for being my "Partner in Life," and Miss Gabor for calling the word to my attention.

BACKGROUND

The Holocaust came late to Hungary and lasted only a short while, from March 19, 1944, to about February 1, 1945. Despite its brevity, it was devastating, killing the largest number of Hungary's 800,000 Jews. Why? Why such senseless brutality? And was it really senseless, the obsession of a madman and his sycophants, or could it have been that the powerful Germans feared a second Warsaw uprising, one that would divert several divisions of troops from the front? This story attempts to correlate survivors' experiences with the historic record of how and why it happened.

Near the River Tisza on the fertile, windy plain of Eastern Hungary stands the village of Büdszentmihaly. In 1750 its recorded Jewish population was only one servant girl. By 1928 its Jewish population had grown to 850, but the harmonious relationship that had existed between Jew and Christian in that village and in the rest of what remained of Hungary had not survived the breakup of the Habsburg Empire.

On Passover, April 14, 1944, 652 Jews were marched from Büdszentmihaly to the death camps. Only 91 of these returned after the war—the rest had perished. By 1975, the recorded Jewish population of Büdszentmihaly was exactly what it had been at the outset: one.

Endre Lowy, my wife's father, came from Büdszentmihaly, where her Uncle Géza was the head of the Jewish community. Géza was among those who went to the ovens. Nor did his wife survive; only two nieces, daughters of other brothers, returned. In 1959, Endre, by now safe in America, returned on a visit to Budapest and to his native village. Physically broken, emotionally spent, he did not live to return to his beloved America. Worse than surviving the terror was facing the resultant devastation, and the memories not only for Endre and the other Jews of Hungary but for the land and its other occupants as well. This is the dilemma that faces emigrés, Jew and Christian alike, who yearn to return, if only for a visit, to their motherland.

Prior to the great war of 1914–18, most of Poland was under Russian Czarist control; the rest remained divided between Hungary and Germany.

The unspeakable poverty of Russified Poland, particularly that among Polish Jews, forced many residents either to leave or to support the forces of revolt that were seething and about to erupt. Of those that fled, many went south to the comparative paradise of Hungary, taking in their midst many radicals.

The revolution that followed the collapse of the Czarist regime swept eastward, and southward. In Hungary, Béla Kun, a Hungarian Jew, had been trained as a revolutionary in Russia herself and had returned to Hungary to seize power and launch a red bloodbath. Determined to halt the spread of Communism, the victorious Allies shut off food supplies to the embattled remnant of a once-proud and powerful Hungary, now reduced by two-thirds, and lent their support to Admiral Nicholas Horthy and his "white" fascist brigades.

By August 1919, Kun had fled, Horthy, the "admiral without a fleet," was in power, and the "white terror" was drenching the execution fields in human blood.

Except for some adventurees, the rank and file of the Hungarian Jews, both native and newly-settled from Poland, opposed Kun and communism no less vigorously than did the "regent," Horthy, who remained in power until he was deposed by Hitler. But the anti-Semites in Hungary made the most of the opportunity provided them by Béla Kun, the Jewish renegade. Anti-Semitism thereby gained official sanction in Hungary. The above is admittedly only a brief simplification of the tragic destruction of a social order that had lasted 200 years. Nevertheless, it must be read as a prelude to an understand-

ing of the tragedy of the Hungarian Holocaust. *I myself was faced with this craving, this need to know about its beginnings.*

The Orient Express that carried my son was due to arrive in Budapest at 8 P.M. Irritated, I glanced at my watch as I sat in the rented Fiat at Hegyeshalom, a border town between Austria and Hungary.

Fifteen minutes had passed and the Hungarian guard still hadn't made a move to lift the iron rail that would allow us to proceed. I glanced at my wife Marianne; her crow's feet seemed deeper; she had a fixed smile at the corners of her mouth, and the furtive look in her green eyes gave away her uneasiness. I had a burning desire to return to Vienna, something that I knew was impossible.

"How did I ever let you talk me into this?" I asked Marianne with a sigh.

"Don't be so impatient," she replied, attempting to console me.

"Damned Communists!"

"It's got nothing to do with Communism," my wife retorted. "What else has the poor guard got to look forward to? Leave him his little pleasures."

Would that I had known then about the Arrow Cross death march a trek of thousands of dehumanized souls to the slave labor corps for Tóth. There I was, parked and waiting for the gate to lift, at the exact place where usable Jews had been transferred to the Germans! The worker-designates were forced to wait like so many cattle on lousy straw, stinking with defecation . . . but the others were less fortunate than they.

Only a few cars waited beyond the gate at the checkpoint (who in his right mind, I wondered, would want to drive into Hungary?), but the road going west toward Austria was clogged with motionless vehicles as far as the eye could see. Cars with hoods raised, trunks open, luggage strewn about everywhere, while police aimed their flashlights (in the bright light of mid-afternoon) behind and above their wheels.

"What national treasures do they expect to find?" I asked, a note of sarcasm in my voice.

"People," was my wife's quiet and simple reply.

At last the gate went up, and I started the engine.

"Don't make me say anything," Marianne cautioned.

I looked at my wife in surprise. "Why not?"

"I don't want they should hear my voice."

"What do you mean?"

"If they hear my accent, they'll know I'm Hungarian."

"But you're an American citizen, you have a U.S. passport!" I protested.

"Next to you that is my most valuable possession," my wife replied. "But. . . ."

I understood her fears. But the border guard was so confused by the combination of Italian license tags and an American driver that, after three trips in and out of his booth, he allowed us to proceed without further ado. While we passed the unbroken line of traffic heading west, I went over recent events in my mind.

Marianne and I were married in 1974. For many years she had borne the burden of being the sole provider for her children. Using skills acquired during her adolescence and given the approval of certification after the liberation, she taught body conditioning to the working rich and to the ambitious young women executives of New York.

Myself a lonesome widower in search of a surrogate mother for my teenaged son, I had met Marianne at a wedding in New York. We felt an instant attraction for each other.

At that time my knowledge of Hungary was limited, and, as a first-generation child of Russian and Polish parents, my understanding of the Hungarian people was influenced by my mother's and father's conflicting interpretations of a nation that was a breed apart. Marianne promptly embarked on a mission to brainwash me. Her method was a simple one: social contact. She kept up a low-keyed but persistent effort to convince me to cross the Iron Curtain with her.

"It wouldn't hurt if once you could see it," was her consistent line of propaganda.

My son was on a student tour of Israel the summer that Marianne and I visited Europe. That is how I, a pharmacist from

Columbus, Ohio, happened to be sitting here in a car bearing Italian license tags the first week of September in 1975, at the very last place in the world that I would have chosen. I was furious with myself for having come at all, at least for not having crossed through the out-of-the-way village of Sopron as a concierge in Austria had advised me to do. It was not an auspicious beginning of our visit.

The trip to Budapest proceeded uneventfully. Many times Marianne warned me of "no camera" signs. Each city and village that we motored through seemed to hold special memories for her, or to recall specific persons who had once resided in the neat, orderly communities whose architecture and peasant homes constantly delighted the eye of her memory. She was happy. The crow's feet grew faint, her verdant eyes sparkled.

I shall give you an example. Györ brought back memories to her of Leslie Geiger, who had stood in our wedding for her father, already dead. Györ was Leslie's birthplace. Marianne quite clearly shared my ignorance about Györ, the marshalling point for Jews from the villages who were forced to join the death march from Budapest; five thousand men, women, and children from nearby Mosonmagyaróvár alone.

But I felt uneasy, dependent upon Marianne to interpret the alphabet-soup road signs, and dusk was already approaching before we approached the Danube. After losing our way for a time we found a bridge that crossed the Danube from the hills of Buda to the flatlands of Pest and I relaxed.

The low ground of Pest was choked with smog from the acrid diesel fuel with its high-sulfur content. The principle thoroughfares had new names now, which made it difficult for Marianne to find her way, but she finally was able to direct me to our hotel, where her childhood friend, who shall be called E., was waiting for us.

E. obviously felt uncomfortable about being seen with us, so we cut our visit short. After we had checked into our room, I explained to Marianne that I had to meet my son at the railroad station; his train due to arrive at 8 P.M. But once we returned to the car, neither Marianne or E. could tell me how to get to the station.

"Don't you even know how to get to the railroad station?" I asked in dismay.

"Yes, but by streetcar." she answered with maddening logic.

After a great deal of consultation, the ladies finally decided that down a certain obscure street on our left, where bright neon lights beckoned, stood the station. But how could we possibly get there? No cars were permitted to cross street-car tracks, one-way streets in the wrong direction: the obstacles seemed insurmountable.

I wheeled the Fiat around anyway and aimed for the lights. Street-car conductors clanged their bells, horns blew, and pedestrians shook their fists at me as they scurried out of the way like a pack of cards in the wind.

"What are you doing?" Marianne protested vehemently. "You'll get us all killed!"

"I'm going to the station, and no, I won't, and they can just all go to hell with their traffic system." I replied, answering her protests in rapid-fire order.

"They'll think you're an ugly American." she persisted.

"No, they won't. With these tags they'll think I'm a crazy Italian. But I'm sure it's okay in Budapest to be a crazy Italian." I blew my horn, waved my arms and forced the issue with several vehicles that blocked our path. E. buried her head between her knees.

Once at the station, Marianne quickly got into a drawn-out argument with the woman in the Ibusz Tourist Office where I had sent her to ask if we had missed the Orient Express from Paris.

"She's unreasonable." my wife fumed.

"No, she isn't; she's mad at you," I replied reasonably, having watched the whole argument from afar.

"Why?" she asked.

"There she sits in her tattered dress doing her thing, and you butt in in your New York clothes. She knew you were Hungarian, but you're the lucky one who got out and she's stuck here."

"Who asked her to stay? She could have got out in '56." Marianned objected.

"Who asked E. to stay?" I replied.

The Orient Express and my son arrived in good order. Ibusz lodged Joe with a family where he slept for the days we were there together.

What with the smog, the police, the food, and the sullen people, I was rapidly developing a strong distaste for Budapest. Marianne took me to visit certain fond places of happy memories from her youth, but war and revolution had left their mark. Although 30 years had passed since the war had ended, virtually every building still displayed its badge of shell holes.

One of the few pleasures that I truly enjoyed turned out to be a visit to their College of Pharmacy, which still retained the customary European tradition of formal relationships between professor and student, despite being a generation behind our own in many other respects.

I also enjoyed observing mothers as they met well-dressed and disciplined school children emerging from their studies. I saw swimming pools a block long, and old, honest-to-goodness Turkish bathhouses. I realized that once, in Budapest, life had been good.

The Jews that I met were a sad lot. E. was typical of them. She conducted herself as if there were a government agent behind every pillar, and as if she would lose her precious teaching position if she were seen in our company. It was the week of the Jewish New Year. Marianne wanted to go to the old Dohany Templom. It was the largest synagogue that I have ever seen. There were two stories of pews for the women (although Marianne sat with me on the main floor). The Ark was magnificent; there was a huge organ, and the lectern stood in the middle of the sanctuary and reminded me of Catholic cathedrals I had visited.

Everywhere that I looked there was dirt. The brass name plates on the seats were black with oxide, the stone floor had not been mopped for thirty years, perhaps longer. The congregation, a conglomeration of solemn people in tattered clothing, filled one-third of the building and were a depressing sight. It was obvious why E. had refused to come.

The old Rabbi gave a non-political, non-religious sermon that Marianne translated for me as best she could.

"How can they keep this beautiful temple in such a state of disrepair?" I asked in amazement.

"All buildings are owned by the government. They don't have a very large budget for synagogues I'm afraid," Marianne answered.

"So why don't the Jews clean it up themselves?"

"Who is left physically able to do it?" she replied simply.

The next day Marianne took me to the old synagogue on Kazinczy Street where her grandfather, her parents and she had worshipped. Here conditions were worse—the Germans had used the building as a stable for their horses. The broken windows had not been replaced; there were few worshippers. I took my place in her grandfather's pew, and she went upstairs to where she had sat with her relatives. It was a very depressing experience.

On Sunday, to fulfill the Jewish tradition between the two High Holy days, Marianne wanted to go to the cemetery. Reluctantly I followed her instructions, driving to the outskirts of Budapest. Eventually we found a Catholic cemetery.

"Fine! Our cemetery is right next to it," Marianne announced triumphantly.

But it wasn't. I doubled back on every path and crossed every road; I approached where it was supposed to be from all directions—no Jewish cemetery was to be found. The Catholic cemetery was well maintained. Marianne asked many people along the way, but no one could direct us.

"The roads have been changed somehow! I know it's here somewhere," she persisted stubbornly.

"Maybe they built a housing project or a factory where it used to be," I suggested. We had gone by both on our wild-goose chase. I wanted to give up, but not Marianne. Finally she let out a scream, "There it is!"

"Where?"

"Over there!"

She pointed across some fields, tall with uncut grass. Sure enough, I could make out headstones.

"It is probably part of the Catholic cemetery."

"No! I see a Star of David. That's it, I tell you! Find the road!"

"If there was a road I would have found it. Hold on!"

I turned the Fiat into the field and plowed my way across.

When we got to the cemetery we found a narrow trail, and I left the car there. The old peasant caretaker had a map of the different plots, and we worked our way through the weeds to her grandfather's grave.

I was interested to know how I could have missed the road, so I didn't drive out where I had entered, but followed the cart path out instead. This route brought us next to a small, yellowish building on the edge of the Catholic cemetery. I remembered having seen it before. Along the driveway stood a small sign with an arrow that pointed back the way we had come.

"There's the sign," I said. "Doesn't it say Jewish Cemetery?"

"No."

"What does it say?"

"Chicken coop," she answered quietly.

Before we left Budapest I suggested that we should buy some of the hundreds of Jewish artifacts, that abounded in the tourist shops and our hotel, The Duna, even though the price tags were outrageous.

"No," she said determinedly.

"Why not?"

"I couldn't stand to look at them."

"Why not?"

"Where do you think they came from?" Even the question seemed to leave a bitter taste in her mouth.

Even if E. did feel sad when Marianne kissed her good-bye, she, the police, and the waiter that charged me twenty-four dollars for an à la carte piece of fish at the Duna Intercontinental Hotel were doubtless relieved to see me head west.

As we approached the only soldier guarding the border at Sopron, I turned to Marianne. "Do you want me to record your story?" I asked.

"Yes," she answered fiercely.

"Why? Every survivor shared your experiences."

"Then everybody should be willing to talk about it."

"Why?" asked Joe from the back seat.

She turned to my son, her voice filled with emotion. "Only if the world remains aware can it prevent the same thing from happening to somebody else."

I pulled up to the border post. The young sentry was only interested in how much currency I had in my pocket.

On the road back to Vienna, I tried to assemble my thoughts about Budapest and its citizens. My eyes, which had for five days been burning from smog, eased a bit, but my heart was still afire with the anger kindled by my experience.

Hungary is a land of strange contrasts, no doubt about it. At night I had looked across the Danube from our window in Pest, facing west through the acrid smog to the hills of Buda where the former palace of the emperor, the cathedral, and the citadel all stood together.

While my eyes gazed at that awesome yet hauntingly beautiful sight, the Kleig lights suddenly went out. It cost too much to keep them burning for more than a few hours a week.

Viewing the three monuments from the other side, I found that only the palace walls remained and that the cathedral had become a tourist attraction alongside a new hotel that Hilton was building. From the shell-ravaged citadel, still standing after five hundred years of war, I looked out over the smog-covered flatland of Pest stretching east as far as the eye could see. I could see clearly that Russia would never voluntarily forfeit this last point of defence.

I now had seen for myself the rich black soil of Hungary. We had gone through mile after endless mile of fields of maize and sunflowers, but I was stunned to see how hundreds upon hundreds of peasants harvested the crops with simple hand scythes and loaded them into horse-drawn, rubber-tired carts.

The hotel dining room had offered no fresh fruit and everything tasted of paprika. I went to a grocery to find out the reason and I saw only a few overripe grapes, a large supply of marmalade (all one flavor), and a massive assortment of alcoholic beverages on the shelves. There was precious little meat or fish, and none of the goose liver that Marianne had assured me she ate by the tablespoonfuls in her youth (we did find the goose liver in the tourist shop, but it was priced at $13 for a half kilo or 1.1 lb.).

But if I abhorred the cuisine of Budapest restaurants, I adored their gypsy cimbalom players. I felt like the snake in a Hindu's basket as those fellows pounded their mallets on the taunt strings so quickly that their fingers were a blur to the eye. And the music was marvelously loud; it had to be loud to be heard over the constant chatter of this soft, phonetic, and rhythmic language of which I understood not a word.

On the streets it was another matter. There was the city at work: the noise of subways abuilding that would also serve as bomb shelters; empty shops; bombed-out buildings staring vacantly. Decay was everywhere, and no one was smiling.

Horthy is gone now, but he symbolized the determination of Hungary to regain respect of the other nations. I think that this determination of the Hungarian people will not be denied.

Marianne does not like to talk about the past A very private person, she does not care to discuss her experiences during the war years. She kept a diary, which is still in her possession, but it tells the outsider nothing because the entries are all code words, meaningful only to her.

Marianne cannot believe that the story of how she and her family survived the war in Budapest, and of the new lives they have made for themselves in the United States and in Canada, would be of interest to those who do not know the Zuckers and the Lowys. I do not share Marianne's view. While much has been written about Jews who spent the Holocaust years in concentration camps or in the underground resistance movement, relatively little has been said at this writing about the Hungarian Jews who survived the Nazi occupation and then the Russian invasion of Hungary, the ones who escaped deportation and were eventually liberated by Russian troops in the ghetto of Budapest. Unlike the Poles and many others, the Jews from the ghetto of Budapest spent less than a year under direct Nazi domination; the hardships they endured were different from those suffered by their fellow Jews who saw torture and death at first hand as a matter of daily routine for three, four, and even five years. Nevertheless, the story of the Jews in Hungary during the Hitler era is not less important a part of the Holocaust history than the accounts now being published in ever-growing numbers by survivors of Auschwitz, Maidanek, Bergen-Belsen, Dachau, or Buchenwald. I believe that the experiences that were related to me, slowly and painfully, by my wife, her mother, her cousins, and other relatives and friends represent a significant contribution to the record of the most tragic era in recent Jewish history.

I have attempted in this book to set down the personal stories that my wife, her relatives and her friends told me. I have made faithful tape recordings of their words, bit by bit, over long periods of time, with much gentle coaxing and prodding. Among the nine distant family members that I have interviewed are Klári and Tibor Vayda, the sister and brother-in-law of Marianne's first husband, the violinist Victor Aitay, and the American members of the Zucker family, who welcomed their Hungarian cousins to New York with open arms, and Tibor Waldman, Pista's partner in Budapest.

I am convinced that Marianne and her relatives owe their survival in large measure to non-Jews, not the least of those Raoul Wallenberg, that valiant, Swedish fighter for justice and humanity, who, at the risk of his own life probably saved tens of thousands of Hungarian Jews from death at the hands of the German Gestapo and the Hungarian "Arrow Cross" gangs. And, so this book is also a humble tribute to the deeds of this man who, it now seems almost certain, ended his life as a martyr somewhere in Soviet Russia.

How could I write about all of this? These were my thoughts as we entered Vienna, and I was suddenly overwhelmed by the contrast. The Nazis and the Russians were once in Vienna, too.

But, above all, the story of Marianne and her family and friends is one of courage, determination and mutual devotion that enabled three generations to live through the Hitler era and to create new lives for themselves in peace. Some of these survivors have lived to see a new generation, born and bred in freedom, a generation which has grown to maturity and is now generously giving of itself to America, the land that provided its parents and grandparents with the reassurance that, as the immortal Anne Frank put it, most people on earth are basically good at heart.

I
Prelude

MARIANNE

Marianne does not look semetic. When I'm in a teasing mood, I hold a scarf across her nose, Oriental-style, look deep into her green eyes, and insist that one of her ancestors was a harem girl left behind by the Turks when they fled post-haste from Budapest in the late 1600s. Who knows how many times Marianne's un-Jewish face saved her life from the Nazis in Hungary? The Holocaust blighted her girlhood and early young womanhood, but Marianne survived.

She was born in Budapest in the mid-1920s. Her parents, Endre (Andrew) and Aranka Zucker Lowy, were well-to-do, pillars of Budapest's worthy, upstanding Orthodox Jewish community. Marianne was their only child. Her early upbringing was a mix of formal adherence to time-honored Jewish laws and customs, *noblesse-oblige* concern for those less fortunate than herself, training in the social skills and graces that were regarded as indispensable for a suitable marriage later on, and the little frivolities that Marianne and her set of friends at the Jewish *gymnasium* took for granted as the just due of girls in their social position during those last carefree years between the two world wars.

The patriarch of the family was Marianne's maternal grandfather, Henrick Zucker. Henrick had come to Budapest from Poland in the late 1860s as an orphan boy with only the training of the traditional *heder*. Together with his wife, Kreindel, who had also come to Hungary from Poland as a child, he built up a china and glassware business which, by the turn of the century, had become the largest of its kind in Central Europe.

In time, Henrick brought most of his older brothers and sisters from Poland to Budapest. Although many of his nephews and nieces were given jobs in the business of Henrick *bácsi*—Uncle Henrick. To most of these relatives, Budapest was just a stopover. Eventually, a niece by marriage, Rickele Padawer Zucker, and her two sons, Nathan and Charles, were the first of the family to settle in the United States. Nathan arrived in New York shortly after World War I. Charles came via France in 1940. Henrick remained a legend of familial benevolence, and the "American" Zuckers proved their gratitude when his daughter Aranka Lowy and his grandchildren, Marianne (Reiss), Zoltan (Weisz) and Eva (Weisz Perkedy, later Korda), arrived in America from Hungary after the Holocaust.

Henrick Zucker survived World War II. He died in Budapest in 1949, at the age of eighty-six. He had outlived Kreindel, who died just before the Depression after World War I that all but ruined him. He survived three of his four daughters. The oldest, Rozsi Weisz, mother of Zoltan and Eva, was killed in Auschwitz. Two younger daughters died long before the war. Olga died from septicemia at the age of sixteen, and beautiful Csilla took her own life.

Henrick's youngest and sole surviving child, Aranka Lowy, became my mother-in-law in 1974.

Marianne's first husband, Pista (Steve) Reiss, who had come with her from Budapest to New York after the war, had died five years earlier. At the time of Pista's death, their son Ronnie, was twenty-two; their daughter, Vivian, eighteen.

MARIANNE

My immediate family in Budapest consisted of my father, Endre Lowy, my mother, Aranka, and myself. Our apartment—we moved there when I was six years old—was on Akafca 6, in one of the most elegant neighborhoods of the city. I think the building had about five or six floors; we lived on the second floor.* There was an elevator, but I never used it. It took less time for me to walk up the steps than to wait for the creaky elevator.

Our apartment was quite large, with three bedrooms, one for my parents, one for me, and one for our maid, Lujza. Each bedroom had a bathroom of its own. Lujza had her own bathroom, too, but her room faced the inner courtyard of our building, while the windows of my parents' bedroom, and my own, faced the street.

I want to tell you more about Lujza. She was our combination cook-and-maid. She first came to us when I was five. She was then a country girl of 17 or 18, unable to read and write, but very goodhearted. She remained with us until I was well into my teens. She had to leave us when the government passed a law forbidding Gentiles to work for Jews as domestics. It was Lujza who saved the gold Marvin watch I received when I graduated from *gymnasium*. I still have that watch. If it hadn't been for Lujza, the Germans would have got it. After the war, Lujza came

*This would be the third floor (according to numbering of American buildings).

to live with Pista—my first husband—and me. One of her sisters was a housekeeper somewhere else in Budapest. I remember that when this woman came to visit Lujza at our apartment before the war, she always brought a little bouquet of flowers for me. There was also a third sister, but she was different from the other two; she was a Communist.

I shared my own room with a succession of nurses and governesses. Until I was three years old, I had a German nurse; so, the first language I learned to speak was not Hungarian but German. This was customary in many Hungarian Jewish homes between the two world wars, and also before. You must remember that until 1918 Hungary was part of the Austro-Hungarian monarchy; so, German was an official language. In fact, many Hungarian Jews of the older generation hardly spoke Hungarian. My grandfather, Henrick Zucker, spoke mostly German at home and did practically all his business in the German language.

When I was older, I got a governess who also lived with us for awhile. In addition to caring for me, and taking me on daily walks to the park, her job was to teach me English. Most of the children my parents knew had some sort of governess or tutor to teach them a foreign language, mostly German, French, or English. As I just said, I already knew German. Why did my mother decide to have me study English rather than French? Perhaps it was the result of a visit we received in Budapest when I was four—distant relatives of ours, Mr. and Mrs. Adolph Zukor, from Hollywood. Mr. Zukor was the famous movie producer. The Zukors were Hungarian-born and were then in Budapest, on a visit to the old country. They came to our apartment for dinner. Much later, I was told that the Zukors were simply overwhelmed by my parents' hospitality, from the shining silver, the beautiful china and the fine crystal down to the initials on our damask table linen—"Z.A." Mrs. Zukor actually believed that Mother had had the tablecloth and napkins initialed especially in honor of Uncle Adolph Zukor! (In Hungary the last name always comes before the first.) She never found out that the initials stood for Mother's maiden name, Aranka Zucker. As a matter of fact, the Zukors weren't even relatives of my mother's. They were related to my father, but I don't exactly remember how.

Anyway, the Zukors apparently were impressed with our apartment, our family—and me. I'm told they asked me whether I would like to come with them to America and act in the movies, like Shirley Temple, who was then the child star of Hollywood. But I wasn't particularly interested; after all, I was only four years old. Before they left, the Zukors urged my mother to have me study English because that was the language of the future. Oh, and in case I ever changed my mind about going to America with them and becoming a movie star, Uncle Zukor would certainly see about getting me a screen role in Hollywood!

To this day I don't know whether my parents really took the Zukors' promise seriously, but Daisy, my English-speaking tutor-governess, first came to us soon after that visit from the Zukors. It isn't hard for a young child to learn a foreign language, and Daisy had a good method. On our daily walks, she'd point to houses, benches, trees and so on, ask me in English, "What is this?" and I'd have to answer, also in English, of course. In about a year's time I spoke English quite well. I hadn't learned to read and write because I was not yet of school age. But later, when I had to learn English spelling, it came to me as if it had been my second nature. I still have my Hungarian accent, but my English spelling, I must say, is quite good.

When I was five, the Zukors visited Budapest again. This time they took me to the theater. We had box seats as befitted a Hollywood movie producer and his party. I loved the performance. But when Uncle Zukor asked me again whether I would like to go with him to America and act in a movie, I told him I'd much rather sit and look at movies than act in them. That month, the cover of *Szinházi élet* (Theater Life), Hungary's well-known theatrical magazine, had a picture showing me, in a checked spring coat, with Mrs. Zukor, elegant in her pearls and furs. The caption read, "Mrs. Adolph Zukor with her niece Marianne." This was the closest I ever got to star billing.

Meanwhile, I continued my English lessons with Daisy. I talked German with my parents at home, and with my grandfather Zucker. The only language I still did not speak then was Hungarian! I didn't really learn Hungarian until I was in the first grade of elementary school.

In Hungary you went to elementary school for four years.
When you graduated, at the age of ten, you could go to grammar
school for four more years. Under the law, you could leave school
when you were fourteen. But children who wanted a better
education moved from the fourth year of elementary school into
gymnasium, an academic high school where they stayed for eight
years. Then they took the *matura*, a kind of comprehensive exam-
ination, which was supposed to prove that the student was sufficiently mature—at least intellectually—to enter a university.

The elementary school I went to was a Jewish day school.
From there, I graduated into the Jewish *gymnasium*, where I
learned yet another language: Hebrew. The Jews in Budapest did
not speak Yiddish—at least not the ones we considered "cultured" and "refined." Even the Orthodox Jews in our city regarded Yiddish not as a language but as a sort of dialect. My father
and mother were proud, observant Jews but even they tended to
be a little snobbish about acting "too Jewish" outside our home.
When my first husband and I came to the United States, we
experienced snobbism working in reverse. The people with
whom Pista began to do business in New York and New Jersey
all spoke Yiddish and looked down on him as something of a *goy*
because they couldn't understand how you could be a Jew from
Europe and not speak Yiddish!

The Jewish *gymnasium* for girls in Budapest was considered a
first-class school. Aside from receiving a thorough education in
the humanities and sciences, we had extracurricular activities,
including a choir and a dramatic club. Our teachers made us very
conscious about how young Jewish ladies should behave. We
were proud of our school uniforms, including the hats with the
emblem of the Jewish *gymnasium*. When you wore that school
hat, whether you were walking in the street, or riding on a bus
or trolley, you knew that you had to behave accordingly. Other
children might scream, or run up and down the streetcar as they
do all over the world. But we couldn't do that; we had to be
well-behaved—better than all the others—because we, the girls of
the Jewish *gymnasium*, were supposed to be the good-will ambas-
sadors of the Jewish people.

After school, there was additional education for me. There were my English lessons, and then lessons in French, piano and physical culture. I went to ballet school five afternoons a week. Those physical culture and ballet lessons were to come in handy for me in the United States, when I myself gave lessons to help support my family.

In the Zucker and Lowy families, education was written in capital letters. My grandfather Henrick Zucker came to Budapest without any worldly schooling. His parents had died and left seven or eight children. Grandfather arrived in Budapest alone, as a boy, and all the education he had was the traditional learning young boys got in the *heder,* the class at the rabbi's house where only Jewish subjects were taught. By the time Grandfather had his own family—four daughters—he was a well-to-do man, in the china and glassware business. He was a very, very pious Jew but also very much interested in modern thought and in the finer things of life. And he wanted his daughters to have the best education possible. So he and Grandmother sent their eldest daughter, Rozsi, and my mother, the youngest, to Jewish boarding schools in Switzerland, where girls from religious, cultured Jewish homes all over Europe got the all-around education that was considered necessary for young Jewish ladies of good breeding. It was mostly training in the lady-like accomplishments: foreign languages, literature, music, and how to be a good Jewish housewife. My Aunt Rozsi (the mother of my cousins Eva and Zoltan Weisz) went to the famous Ascher boarding school in Montreux; Ascher's was so well known among religious Jews all over the world that children were sent there even from as far away as the United States. My mother went to another boarding school, in Neufchâtel. I didn't know my grandmother Kreindel; she died when I was about two and a half. When I was ten or so, my grandfather remarried. His second wife, Hilda, was an educated woman, a licensed teacher of English, French, and German. She was much younger than my grandfather; she only died in 1976, in Budapest.

We always spent the Jewish holidays at Grandfather's house. I often heard about the fabulous dinners he gave on the holiday of Purim—that celebrates Queen Esther and the downfall of the wicked Haman, who wanted to kill the Jews. All the poor Jews in Budapest were invited. The cook would start preparations four weeks earlier—the turkeys, pastries, and the rest of it. On Purim day, it was open house. One of my mother's uncles would stand at the door of Grandfather's apartment and let the guests in. All the furniture was moved out of the rooms and long tables had been set up in every room. That way they'd serve dinner to about 300 people, in shifts of 25 or 30. Grandfather was known far and wide for his good works. I don't think many people of his kind exist today.

CHARLES ZUCKER

Charles Zucker, of New York City, is a grandnephew of Marianne's grandfather, Henrick Zucker. He is a grandson of Henrick's brother Mendel. Translated into simpler *mishpokhology*, this means that Charles' father, Benjamin, and Marianne's mother, Aranka Lowy, were first cousins.

Since the death of his older brother, Nathan (who came to the United States soon after World War I), Charles, who is now almost eighty, has been considered the leader of the Zucker clan. Arriving in New York by way of France in 1940, Charles became a prosperous businessman. He never forgot the help that Uncle Henrick, in Budapest, gave to his mother, Rickele, when she fled from Poland to Hungary during World War I.

Charles and his sister's husband, Jack Friedman, were among the first Jews from the West to visit Hungary after the Holocaust, to seek out the surviving members of Uncle Henrick's family and to offer them help.

I was born in 1905, in Mielec. That's in Poland. My mother, Rickele, was an exceptionally good businessman; I think she began working at the age of twelve. In Mielec, about 90 percent of the town's Jews made a living from the sale of feathers; so did our family. We mostly got our raw material from the *shochetim*, the ritual slaughterers who killed chickens and geese. But there was a lot of competition and my father, Benjamin Zucker, decided to go to Paris. Paris in those days was the world market for feathers. But he didn't consider Paris a good place for raising a

Jewish family, so it was agreed that my mother and we children should stay in Mielec while my father did business in Paris and sent the money home. This meant that my mother had to take care of six, and eventually seven young children, and run the household all by herself. My father came home to Mielec only twice a year: in the spring for Passover, and again in the fall for Rosh Hashanah and Yom Kippur. This went on for quite a few years.

Then, in 1914, when I was nine, World War I broke out. Because our hometown, Mielec, was part of the old Austro-Hungarian Empire, my father, in France, because an enemy alien and was taken to an internment camp. Meanwhile, my mother and we seven children were stuck in Mielec. My mother decided to go to Switzerland, which was neutral, and take with her a substantial amount of money. She heard that, from Switzerland, she might be able to bribe the French authorities and they might let my father out. She left us children behind in Mielec in the care of her sister.

But then the war came to Mielec. The Russians came closer and closer. My aunt, like many others in town, decided we'd better run away. So she hired a horse and wagon, piled us, and as many belongings as possible, into the wagon, and so we left Mielec, moving westward, away from the Russians. But where were we to go? Some Jews from Mielec headed for Czechoslovakia, or Germany, or a big city like Vienna. My aunt said we were going to Budapest, because that's where my father had an uncle, Henrick Zucker, who was rich, and famous for his good deeds.

Meanwhile, my mother never made it to Switzerland. She tried to go back to Mielec, but she never got there either; the Russian troops were advancing too fast. But somewhere, on the highway, she met people from our town. They told her, "Your children left Mielec with your sister in a horse and wagon. They probably went either to Vienna or to Hungary." My mother guessed right away that my aunt must have taken us to Budapest, to our uncle Henrick Zucker.

I don't remember all the details, but when we arrived in Budapest we found that Uncle Henrick had taken into his home maybe fourteen or eighteen young relatives who had fled from Poland. All of these relatives were orphans, mere children; I think the oldest in the lot was fourteen.

Unlike many other people who started out poor and then became rich, Uncle Henrick took pride in his humble beginnings. Every time he made a speech at some charitable organization, he'd tell how he came to Budapest from his hometown in Poland with holes in his shoes. And he never, never was ashamed of his poor relatives whom he settled in Budapest over the years. He got jobs for everybody, mostly in his own business. He'd marry off the girls—this meant finding the right man, a dowry, and an apartment for the young couple.

In 1910 or so, Uncle Henrick had trouble with his business. There was a big fire in his warehouse, where he kept the china and glassware he'd imported from all over Europe. The warehouse, and everything in it, burned down to the ground. He didn't have enough insurance, but even so, some anti-Semitic people spread the rumor that Henrick had set the fire himself to get the insurance money. As a result, Henrick was arrested and sat in jail for a couple of weeks. But then he was cleared of having had anything to do with the fire and the insurance paid the money that was coming to him. The next important Jewish holiday after that fire was Yom Kippur, the Day of Atonement. Henrick was a prominent member of the big Orthodox synagogue in Budapest; I think he was even president of the congregation for a time. Anyway, for that Yom Kippur, he bought himself an *aliyah*, the honor of being called to read from the Torah. When he was called to the reading platform, he stood up and swore in front of the open Ark of the Law that he had not set the fire to his warehouse. He wanted the whole Jewish community to know that he was really innocent. He was the fifth man to be called to the Torah on that Yom Kippur, and he made a custom of it; every year thereafter, for Yom Kippur, he reserved the fifth *aliyah* for himself.

When my father, in Paris, heard of Uncle Henrick's trouble with the warehouse, he sent him some money to help him build up his business again. By the time World War I broke out,

Henrick was in good shape again. When we children arrived in Budapest from Mielec, he took an apartment for us near his new warehouse, just outside the city. Eventually, my mother also made it to Budapest. But what was she going to do? My father was still interned somewhere in France, and the money she'd brought with her from Mielec wouldn't last forever. So she paid a visit to Uncle Henrick and asked him to help her start some small business.

Uncle Henrick didn't hesitate for a moment. "Rickele," he said to my mother, "your credit with me is good. You were always a smart businesswoman. Besides, your husband sent me money when I was in trouble. So, if you need money, now to go into business for yourself, it'll be my pleasure to help you."

Mother did engage in business while she was in Budapest—the feather business—and repaid all the money Uncle Henrick had lent her.

In 1917 the Russians were being pushed back on the Eastern front, so Mother and all of us children went back to Mielec. All of us, that is, except my brother Nathan, who was five years older than I. When we first came to Budapest, Nathan was fourteen years old and felt very grown-up. When our great-uncle Henrick tried to play father to him, he resented it and tried to make money on his own by selling cigarettes to soldiers on the black market. Once in a while Nathan ran away from home. Then Mother would run to Uncle Henrick and ask him to help her find Nathan. One time, Uncle Henrick found Nathan in the old Jewish section of Budapest, sleeping in a synagogue because he didn't have the money for a hotel room. Uncle Henrick didn't know much about psychology. He just gave Nathan two swats and took him home. This only made Nathan even more angry. He went around with Béla Kun's Communist gang that ran Hungary for a while around 1919. Later, he stopped being a Communist, left Hungary and went off to Vienna.

Meanwhile the war had ended and my father came home from Paris to Mielec. When he heard that Nathan was in Vienna, my father went to Vienna, found my brother and made him a proposition. "I want to go back to Paris and get our feather business going again," he said. "You come with me, Nathan, and help me." Nathan accepted the offer and went to Paris with my father, but it didn't work out. Nathan was nineteen by then, going on twenty, and couldn't get used to having his father tell him what to do and what not to do.

Eventually, Nathan decided to go to America. Father and his friends tried very hard to talk him out of it. In those days, it wasn't considered such a good idea among Jewish businesspeople in Europe to pull up stakes and go to America. Your father is making good money, his friends told Nathan. Why should you go to America? But Nathan was not to be talked out of his plan, and so, off he went to New York.

In New York, Nathan went from one feather business to another to find a job. Actually, he didn't know a thing about feathers, but he made believe he did. This, and the fact that many of the Jewish feather dealers in New York knew about Benjamin Zucker's business in Paris, made it hard for Nathan. The feather people were all afraid that Nathan wouldn't stay long in any job but would set up his own business and go into competition with them.

Finally, Nathan did find a job—with a feather man who'd come from Europe himself and had once worked for our father in Paris. This man proudly wrote home to his family in Poland, "You know who's working for me now? You wouldn't believe it— Benjamin Zucker's son!"

Back in Paris, our father was still angry at Nathan for having left home. "I need you in Paris," he used to write to him. "What great things can you do in New York that you couldn't do here with me?" But before long, Nathan began to write letters to our father: "Send me feathers from Paris. I can get rich here." Father was still angry, but he started sending the feathers to New York, and soon Nathan really became a very successful businessman. And Nathan, who had been such a tough customer back in Paris, turned out to an exceptionally good son. He couldn't do enough for his mother, his brothers and sisters in Poland, and for his father in Paris. He called his father almost every week from New York although overseas calls in those days, the 1920's, cost a lot of money.

During those early years after World War I, the family was still separated. Father was in Paris, while Mother and the rest of us, except Nathan, were in Mielec. Father said he was afraid to bring the family to Paris because the children would become regular *goyim* in France. In Poland, he said, it was easier for young Jews to remain religious. But I think the real reason for this arrangement was financial. My mother was an extremely big asset to the family business. She had become a real expert in feathers and knew how to select the kind of merchandise in Poland that would sell in Paris.

After a while, I joined my father in Paris. In the end, my mother insisted that the whole family should be together, and so all of us Zuckers left Mielec for France. The business was now expanding rapidly. We started importing feathers from China— ostrich feathers from Africa, and other kinds we had not handled before. And we had steady contact with Nathan in New York, who came over to Paris twice each year to see the family and to go over plans for the business.

Later, I left the family business and tried something on my own, not at all related to feathers. But then, in 1935, Father died and, out of family piety, I suppose, I returned to the family business. In 1938, I took over.

By that time Nathan was writing to my mother and me that we should leave Paris and come to New York because it was clear to him that Europe would soon be at war.

In the spring of 1938, after the German Anschluss of Austria, my wife Lottie—I had married in the meantime—and I gave in to Nathan's urgings and visited America to see whether we would want to live there permanently.

In New York, Nathan gave us a big reception and took me around the city to introduce me to his friends. He tried to convince me to remain in New York. But I insisted on going back to France. You see, I was in the French army reserves. Nathan couldn't understand why I should want to go back and be a soldier in the French army. But I told him that the French would probably soon go to war against Hitler and it was my duty, as a French Jew, to join that fight. How could I face my father's grave if I ran away to America in order to stay out of the war against the Nazis?

So I returned to Europe. But at the same time I started sending money from Paris to a bank in New York so I should have some cash in the United States just in case we would be forced to leave France.

EVA WEISZ KORDA

Eva Weisz Korda is Marianne's first cousin. Eva's mother, Rozsi
Zucker Weisz, and Marianne's mother, Aranka Zucker Lowy, were
sisters. Rozsi was the oldest, Aranka the youngest. Like Marianne,
Eva, too; married her first husband in 1944; after the Germans had
occupied Budapest. Eva, a sculptor and artist, is now living in
Toronto, Canada, with her second husband, Martin Korda. The
Kordas have two sons, Andy and Jeffrey.

I am older than my cousin Marianne. Marianne and I are good
friends, but aside from the fact that we were both born in Budapest and had the same grandparents on our mothers' side—Henrick and Kandel Zucker—our backgrounds are very different.

First of all, Marianne was an only child. I was the youngest of
three. There is my oldest brother, Zoltan, who is now living in
Queens, New York. Another brother, Bandi (the English would
be Andrew), was two years younger than Zoltan; he died in
Dachau, only a few days before the camp was liberated.

Marianne's father, my uncle Endre Lowy, was in business; he
worked on the stock market and dealt in real estate on the side.
Her mother, my aunt Aranka, was working as a travel agent even
then, back in Budapest during the 1930s. (Today, in her late
seventies, she's still a travel agent in New York.) My father, Mör
Weisz, was a landowner. We owned a farm—an estate, about
2,000 acres of land—in Szabolcsbaka, a village in eastern Hungary. This village had a total population of about 1,000. We would

spend the summer and fall seasons—from about the end of May until November—on the estate. During the winter we lived in the city. Until I was ten, "the city" was Budapest. After that, it was Nyiregyháza, which was much closer to the estate. Nyiregyháza, which wasn't too far from the Czechoslovakian Rumanian border, was a fairly large city, with a population of about 65,000. About ten percent of the population was Jewish.

Marianne used to visit us at our estate almost every summer; she'd stay with us about a month. We also spent a lot of time together in Budapest as long as my parents lived there in the winter. After we moved to Nyiregyháza, we saw each other every three or four months.

Marianne was raised like a little princess; I don't think she really met any poor people. When she came to Szabolcsbaka, it was just a grand vacation for her—playing tennis, going swimming, having fun. But I was there almost half of each year, and I saw the less pleasant side of living in the country. I was very much concerned about how the peasants lived. I used to visit them in their houses, and many times I came home barefooted, because I'd left my shoes behind for the peasant children. Often I'd also leave an apron, or whatever other clothing I didn't need. At home, I'd tell my parents I'd lost it, whatever it was. I always felt sorry for those poor people.

I don't know whether Marianne as a little girl gave much thought to what she would like to become when she grew up. I suppose she took it for granted that she would get married and have a child or two. I was different; you might say I started out on my life's work even before I was of school age. I am a painter and sculptor today, and I first began to draw with crayons when I was five or six. Most of those early pictures showed how we lived on our farm—the wheat, the tobacco, the potatoes, the animals. . . .

The troubles began in 1938. That was the time after the Munich Agreement, when Chamberlain sold out Czechoslovakia to the Germans, and Hungary got back large areas she'd been forced to give up to Czechoslovakia after World War I. The Hungarians became very patriotic; all kinds of nationalist groups grew up, like the so-called "freedom fighters'" movement. A lot of these gangs expressed their Hungarian "patriotism" by roaming the country-side, looting Jewish homes and destroying Jewish property. They didn't try it in the cities at the time, because the police there kept order, but they did plenty of damage in the villages, where the local police simply looked the other way.

The "freedom fighters" made a stop also at our village, Sza-bolcsbaka. My parents, my brother Bandi, and I got into our car and drove off to Budapest. Meanwhile, the "freedom fighters" killed all our cattle and horses, set our stables on fire and de-stroyed everything inside our home.

ZOLTAN WEISS

Zoltan Weiss, brother of Eva Weisz Korda and first cousin of Marianne, is a semi-retired textile designer in Queens, New York, where he lives with his wife, Helen. His two children are grown. Devoutly Orthodox, Zoltan is active in Jewish communal work and devotes much time and concern to his aunt, Aranka Zucker Lowy.

I was born in 1915, in the middle of World War I. By the early 1930s I could already feel the bad winds of a new war blowing. I wasn't interested in agriculture or working on my father's estate. My brother Bandi, who was two years younger than I, loved farming and studied briefly at an agricultural college, but it was an anti-Semitic place; the students and instructors started acting up against the Jews and Bandi quit. I never wanted to go into farming. I was sure that, sooner or later, we'd all have to leave Hungary, so I wanted to have a skill or trade I could use anywhere—America, Australia, Palestine. That's why I chose textiles. I went to Vienna to study at a textile school from 1935 to 1936. Then, in December 1937, I opened a small textile mill of my own just outside Budapest, together with a partner, Imre Bodonyi. Imre and I worked with the material known as *loden*, a coarse, shaggy woolen cloth. What I really wanted to do was go to Palestine. In fact, my aunt Aranka Lowy went on a visit to Palestine early in 1938, and enrolled my brother Bandi and me— in absentia—at the Haifa Technion, but my father did not want to let us go. He said he didn't raise his sons so that they should live so far away from him. My father was a clever, intelligent man, but somehow, like many other Hungarian Jews at that time, he lacked foresight. He was convinced that nothing could happen to the Jews in Hungary—not even later that year, after our farm was looted by the Hungarian "freedom fighters." My Aunt Aranka, perhaps, saw things more clearly, but even she returned to Hungary from Palestine!

Horthy worked hard to reestablish Hungary, now independent of Austria, but deprived of land and great segments of Hungarians, apportioned to neighboring countries. He sought an opportunity to capitalize on the upheaval that Hitler was causing, in order to regain lost territories. After the 1936 German Olympics, he actively courted Hitler. By March 11, 1938 and the Austrian Anschluss by Hitler, he expected dividends. In 1938, Horthy accepted the first major anti-Jewish since the infamous 1920 XXV Law of "Numerous Clausus," linking Jewish University professional enrollment to population percentages. This law limited to twenty percent (then to six percent) the number of Jews in certain professions. And made race (Jewish) the criterion of religion.

After the 1938 Munich Agreement, his loyalty paid off with the return of upper Hungary. In March of 1939 Hitler tore up the Munich Agreement, and Horthy demanded and received Ruthenia to the north, reestablishing Hungary's common border with Poland, reasoning that people can commit suicide, a nation cannot.

Part of Hitler's price was further anti-Semitic measures, and entry into the war by Hungary, which came in April of 1941.

In January 1942, 1300 Hungarian innocents, mostly Jews, were murdered and thrown into the Danube.

In April 1943, Hitler had his first Schloss Klessheim meeting with Horthy. Von Ribbentrop demanded (that) Jews be killed or sent to concentration camps. Horthy countered on humanitarian grounds, which frustrated Goebbels. Hitler sent Veesenmayer to Hungary to initiate active measures against the Jews. The days of the final solution program were nipping the Hungarian legs, although Horthy was looking for a way to withdraw from a losing war.

ARANKA ZUCKER LOWY

Aranka Zucker Lowy, Marianne's mother and the youngest and only surviving child of Henrick Zucker, is the unquestioned matriarch of the Zucker clan today—including the "American" members of the family.

She is kind, generous, and one of the shrewdest people I have ever known. She worked as a travel agent in Budapest when most women of her social position considered it a little unsuitable for a married woman in comfortable circumstances to work. Almost immediately upon her arrival in New York in 1947, she resumed her work as a travel agent. Today, at almost eighty years of age, Aranka is still in the travel business.

During the years immediately following World War II, Aranka brought Holocaust survivors from Hungary to the United States by any means—so much so that at one point our State Department declared her *persona non grata*. She ignored the writ and continued saving lives. Over 200 Hungarian Jews owe their escape from behind the Iron Curtain to the help of Aranka Lowy.

Before the Germans came, we had a very nice life in Budapest —my husband, Endre Lowy, my daughter Marianne and I. We had a fine apartment in Budapest, and long, leisurely summer vacations visiting our relatives in the country or swimming and boating at Siofok—a resort on Lake Balaton, very popular with Hungarian Jews or in the early years Carlsbad, where my father had a large glass and china business.

My husband Endre was thirty-six years old when we married.

He was a cultured man, a lover of music and the theater. In his youth he studied medicine, but his experiences in World War I, as a medical orderly disillusioned him. He was the president of the Commodity Exchange but I think I enjoyed the business world more. I had worked as a child in my father's business. So during the Depression of the 1930s I thought that maybe I could help out. One day, on the beach, a friend of mine said to me, "You know so much about other countries. Why don't you become a travel agent?" I did, and that has been my business to this day.

In the spring of 1938 I organized a trip to Palestine for a group of 35 people, including the President of the Zionist Organization of Budapest. I acted as tour leader and guide. I didn't want to live in Palestine myself. I thought that if Endre, Marianne, and I would ever be forced to leave Hungary, we'd go to the United States. My cousin, Nathan Zucker, was already there. The difficulties and hardships I saw in Palestine on my visit that spring convinced me that the place wouldn't be for me. Maybe I was spoiled: I preferred the comforts I enjoyed at home—most of the people in the tour found ways of staying in Palestine, but I returned to Budapest.

However, I thought that my nephews, Zoltan and Bandi Weiss, would do very well in Palestine. So, while I was there, I registered them as students at the Haifa Technion. But when I came back to Hungary and told them what I had done for them, their parents—my sister Rozsi and my brother-in-law Musu— were unhappy. They didn't like it. Musu said, "No! Hitler will never come to Hungary. Rozsi and I will not leave. If the boys want to go to Palestine, they can go, but we'd rather have the family stay together here, at home in Hungary." In the end Zoltan and Bandi didn't go, and of course neither did Rozsi and Musu. Six years later, as Musu got on the deportation train with Rozsi and their son Bandi—he was already on the steps of the car —he handed a letter to somebody in the station to send to me.

"Dear Aranka," he wrote. "I am sorry I did not listen to you back in 1938. I don't know where Rozsi and I are going, but you have our older son and our daughter still with you, in Budapest. Please save them if you can. If I was in your position, I would do the same for your daughter Marianne." Well, I was able to save two of my sister's children, Eva and Zoltan. And not a day passes that Zoltan doesn't call me. He and his wife, Helen, treat me like a mother and Eva too, is like my daughter.

PAULINE METZGER

The apartment of Pauline Metzger, the American sister-in-law of
Charles Zucker (she is the widow of his brother Nathan), on New
York's West Side has always been open to Marianne and the rest of
the Zucker clan. Marianne and I were married there in 1974, and
whenever we are in New York, Pauline expects us at the weekly
family gatherings she holds each Saturday afternoon.

Nathan Zucker died before I met Marianne. Not long after our
wedding, Pauline remarried; her new husband was Morris Metzger.
Unfortunately Morris, too, has died.

When my husband's brother, Charles, came from France to
visit us in New York in 1938 my husband, Nathan—may he rest
in peace—begged him to dissolve his business in Paris and come
to live in America. But Charles insisted on going back to France.
Not long after that, Nathan and I made a trip to Europe—to Paris
and from there to Prague. Strangely, the people we met on our
trip didn't seem nearly as worried as we were about the future.
On the train from France to Prague (Hitler hadn't taken over
Czechoslovakia as yet) we met a man from Berlin. When you are
on a long train ride you tend to strike up conversations with other
passengers. The man told us that he was going to Carlsbad for a
ten-day cure. The German authorities had given him permission
to make the trip, but he admitted that he had trouble getting
money out of his bank in Berlin; he had to show them a certificate
from his doctor. He also mentioned that his little daughter, a girl

of ten, couldn't go to public school anymore. The Germans didn't want Jewish children in public schools. So he had to put her into a private school, at great expense.

Listening to all this, we asked him, "Why don't you leave Germany for good?" He must have been a man not much over forty. He answered, "My dear friends, you know how it is . . . you live in a country, you have a business, your children were born there . . . you can't just pick up and go." Nathan was really upset. "Are you so blind that you can't see what's coming?" he asked the man. "What are you waiting for? Get out of Germany before it is too late." But the man did not answer; he just gave a sad smile. I'm sure that poor soul eventually ended up in a concentration camp.

Nathan and I went to Prague but we stayed for only a short time. Then we returned to France and boarded a boat back to New York.

The following year, World War II broke out.

EVA

Until World War II broke out in September 1939 Jewish boys in Hungary were called into the military reserves just as all other young Hungarian men. Hungary didn't enter the war, but the Horthy government didn't want to offend the Germans. By 1940 all Jewish boys had been expelled from the Hungarian army, and they were subject to being drafted for service in special labor camps. One of these young men was the man I later married. My two brothers, Zoltan and Bandi, took their share.

CHARLES

When the war broke out, I was a reservist in the French army.
Three or four days before war was declared, I received a sum-
mons from the French military authorities to report at a certain
place, with my car, to provide transportation for officers. I left my
family in Paris and went where I was told. Immediately, the army
people gave me an officer to chauffeur around. At first, I wasn't
too unhappy. But very quickly I found out that the company to
which I'd been assigned was a penal battalion. Most of the men
in it were criminals. If you were sentenced to do time in prison
for certain offenses, you could avoid jail if you joined the army.
At any rate, I found out that the men in my company were really
tough babies. I didn't feel it too badly in the beginning, when I
still had my own car and was driving only the officers. But later
they took away my car and gave me a truck instead. They wanted
me to learn to drive a truck so I could get a truck driver's license.
At that point I realized that the men in my company, including
myself, were considered expendable. Before we knew it, we were
right on the battlefront, at the Maginot Line. We had to transport
plenty of munitions—bombs and other such deadly weapons. We
knew that if anything at all went wrong, our whole company
would be blown up.

Before I left Paris, I made arrangements with one of the employees in my feather business to get my family out of the city,
to a small place—Cosne in the province of Nièvre, so they'd be

safe from air raids. The family: this meant my mother, my sisters, my wife Lottie, our two little daughters, and Lottie's family. That was a lot of people. My wife came from a big, well-known Jewish family, the Gutwirths in Antwerp. By the time the war broke out, most of my in-laws were living in France, and they all wanted to be together. But I didn't think they should all live together in one house, so I gave my man some money to rent separate apartments for my in-laws, my sister-in-law, and the others. That came to eight separate apartments, but I was willing to pay for them all. The way I saw it, the more separate apartments we had, the more peace there would be in the family.

After a while it occurred to me that my wife and the children shouldn't live in the same town as her parents. They didn't get along so well because the Gutwirths were very, very pious—my mother-in-law still wore a *sheitel*, the old-fashioned wig for Orthodox married women—but Lottie was a little more modern. One of the men in my company told me he had a house in a place called Chatellerault near Poitiers where Lottie and our two daughters could live very nicely. They made the move and I sent them much food for their own use, and for barter—but only some of it reached them.

The war in France didn't even last a year. The Germans took all of northern France and my wife and the rest of the family had to flee for their lives. I heard that they'd made it to Vichy, but I had no way of getting in touch with them because our company was on the move all the time, retreating from the Germans.

I was then a truck driver's helper. My "boss" was a young Jewish boy named Dreyfus, who'd joined the army to get out of a three-year prison sentence. When we came close to Vichy with our truck, I said to Dreyfus, "I want to stay here a little longer to find out where my family is." But we weren't allowed to stop for any reason. So I said to Dreyfus, "Let's get our truck into some kind of accident so we'll be able to stop. Drive into a tree, or whatever—I don't care what you do, I want to get in touch with my family." Dreyfus decided that would be too risky; he had a better idea. He'd put sand into the motor to make the truck stop.

Whenever we were ready to move on, he'd take the sand out again or, if that didn't work, he'd ask for another truck.

So we used the sand and arranged for a little "breakdown." We abandoned the truck and I went to the Vichy post office to put in a call to the kosher restaurant in town. Since my father-in-law was strictly Orthodox, I figured they'd know his whereabouts at the kosher restaurant. As it happened, my father-in-law himself came to the phone. I told him where I was, and soon Lottie and my sister were with me. I said to them, "I'm not sure the Germans won't come here, too. I can't stay with you. I have to move on with my company. But don't try to flee. You can't imagine what's going on all over the highways—children dying, people and animals running for their lives. It'll be better for you to stay where you are now. Better take your chances with the Germans than get trampled or machine-gunned on the highway."

But Lottie's family didn't want to stay in Vichy. They were afraid that if the Germans came, all the young men and boys would be deported. So they decided to go south, to the Pyrenees, near the Spanish border. From there, they hoped to be able, eventually, to get into Spain.

By accident—or perhaps by good fortune—our company got orders to move in the same direction: to the south. When we finally came to a stop, I got hold of some newspapers. The papers didn't contain a lot of news; they were censored. But they were full of ads—families looking for each other. So I also gave an ad to one paper saying that my company and I were stationed in such and such a place and that we were looking for our wives and children and other relatives. Some woman contacted Lottie and told her about the ad. She came to me; you can imagine the reunion! I told her I wanted to have my mother, my sisters, and the Gutwirths all together. Then we could decide what to do next. Most of the French soldiers were deserting; they didn't bother about applying for a discharge. After all, the war had ended for France. But I didn't want to desert; I said a Jew had no business leaving the French army without legitimate discharge papers.

It didn't take long for me to get discharged. Then I joined

Lottie and other members of the family in the Pyrenees. My sisters, I found out, were in Nice.

I said to Lottie, "I'm disappointed in France. I can't see us staying here. Let's get out of the country while we can."

In order to get out, of course, we had to have passports. So the very next Monday I went to the local police to ask about passports. Since this was a very small town, we received our passports one—two—three. But we discovered we weren't through yet. Our passports weren't valid unless we had exit visas stamped into them. And you couldn't get an exit visa without the approval of the authorities. The place where we were was in Unoccupied France, but the French authorities there weren't all that much better than the Germans. However, luck was with us and we got around that difficulty, too. Soon we all had valid passports.

Now the whole family, Zuckers and Gutwirths, went to Nice. Nice was once a ritzy seaside resort on the French Riviera, but then the hotels were full of refugees, almost all of them Jewish, waiting to see what country would take them in before the Germans caught up with them. Part of the Gutwirth family eventually ended up in South Africa. I got in touch with my brother Nathan in New York. After a while Nathan sent us a cable, telling us that my mother, my wife and children, my sister, and I could come to America on special emergency visas. President Roosevelt had set aside a few hundred visas for Jewish refugees who were considered important—famous rabbis, scholars, presidents of big organizations—and Nathan had managed to get us on the list. By this time we had a third child, a boy, whom we named Benny after my late father.

When we left Nice late in the summer of 1940, Benny was only six months old. Our first stop was Lisbon, in Portugal. There, we had to wait over two months before we could get space on a boat for America. But finally we were able to leave. I still remember the name of our boat, the S.S. *Serpa Pinto*. We traveled first class, but there were six of us in a cabin meant for only one person: Lottie and myself, my mother and our three children. When we wanted to get undressed for bed, we had to step out of the cabin.

But we forgot about all this when we landed in New York. I

can't find words to describe the welcome we were given by my brother Nathan. He and his wife Pauline were then living on the West Side—West 86th Street, with all the other wealthy Jews. He wanted to get apartments for my mother, and for Lottie and me, in the same building. But at the time you couldn't get two apartments in the same house in that neighborhood; it was hard at the time to find an apartment in any nice Manhattan neighborhood. Finally, Nathan found two apartments on the Grand Concourse, but that was in The Bronx, not quite so high-class as the West Side of Manhattan. And my brother Nathan—what a man! He didn't want to stay on the West Side when his mother and his brother were far away, in The Bronx. So he and Pauline also moved to The Bronx, into the same building on the Grand Concourse. What they didn't tell us was that at the same time they kept on paying rent for their old apartment on the West Side because they couldn't break their lease.

Even before I had an apartment, I had a job. When we got off the boat, Nathan told me that he was making me a fifty percent partner in his feather business, with the same rights as he had—everything.

After about a year, all of us left The Bronx. Nathan and Pauline —who'd just had a baby—moved back to their place on West 86th Street, and the rest of us found apartments near them. That's where we were when Marianne and Zoltan and the rest of our Hungarian relatives arrived in New York after the war.

ZOLTAN

In 1938 our farm in Szabolcsbaka was looted. Three years later, we lost our farm officially under the so-called "Jewish laws." The Hungarian government started passing "Jewish laws"—anti-Jewish restrictions—as early as 1938 under Prime Minister Kálmán Darànyi but the new set of laws that came out in 1941 and 1942 was much worse. Jews couldn't own landed property. Also, the government put a "Jewish quota" on certain higher positions in industry and banking. Since the Jews made up about six percent of Hungary's total population, the government said that only six percent of all the executives in banks and factories could be Jews.

I still had my textile mill in Budapest, but it was getting harder and harder for my partner and me to obtain the material we needed. In the beginning, I managed to stay out of labor camp; my family had connections, and I was able to fake sickness, so I was in and out.

Things became more difficult after the Germans attacked Russia in June of 1941. The Hungarians hadn't entered the war yet but they were asked to help the Germans, and labor camp inmates were sent from Hungary to the Russian front for such jobs as digging trenches. Most of the Hungarian officers and sergeants who bossed the help from the labor camps were quite brutal. Also, labor camp inmates were not allowed to carry any weapons, not even when they were put to work close to the battle lines. So they couldn't defend themselves; I don't know how many of them were killed by bombs or shells.

By that time it was quite hard for young Hungarian Jewish men to avoid being drafted for labor service. I was caught, too, but because of my family's connections, I managed to get a reprieve from labor service before they could send me to the battlefront. Even if you were in a labor camp, you could take certain privileges if you had a little money. For instance, you could ask for short furloughs to go into town, making up some story about having to go to your family doctor for a shot, or to visit your sick wife or your dying father. An orderly would escort you to town and then bring you back again to the camp.

You still could perform such tricks then because the Germans, at least officially, were still not in Hungary. The Holocaust had not as yet begun for us—not yet.

MARIANNE

I first met my husband, Pista Reiss, in Budapest, in the spring of 1943. I was not yet eighteen; I was in my last year at the Jewish *gymnasium*. My father was working in real estate then, and Pista came to our apartment to ask his advice about a building he wanted to buy. In retrospect, can you imagine—as late as 1943 there were Jews in Budapest who bought houses and in general lived as if the Nazis and the war were thousands of miles away!

At any rate, my father came into my room that day and said there was a gentleman in the parlor who wanted very much to meet me. I said I was too busy studying for my *matura* examinations, but my father insisted that I come out and meet Mr. Reiss.

I didn't fall in love with Pista at first sight. He was twelve years older than I. So, like a well brought-up young lady I introduced myself to our guest and then went back to my room. Studying for the *matura* exams took months; there was no time to waste.

But Pista started to phone me. Finally, I agreed to go out with him. On our second date he asked me to marry him. I thought this was very funny and laughed right in his face. "Why don't you ask me again six months from now on my birthday?" I suggested. "Then I'll see what my answer will be."

In June 1943, our class passed the *matura*. We celebrated our graduation with a night out on the town. It was all very innocent, of course, because this was an all-girl school and the only gentlemen present were our teachers. We rented a well-known restaurant in the Buda section; the place had a romantic atmosphere, with an outdoor garden and marvelous food.

When we got there, we found a case of champagne waiting for us—a gift to my class from Pista Reiss.

It was a wonderful evening—a gourmet dinner, the champagne chilled just right, and, as our guest of honor, my favorite teacher, Professor Joseph Turoczi-Trostler. He taught Hungarian literature. He was a jolly fellow but in a way frustrated. He was a university-level professor but it had always been hard for a Jew in Budapest to get a university professorship, so he had to settle for teaching at a girls' high school. Sometimes he forgot we were only high school girls and his lectures were a little high-hat, but he had some girls that he liked very much—and vice versa. I was one of them.

We were in high spirits that evening. We started out at the restaurant and then went on to other places. Most of the night, properly chaperoned, of course, we marched up and down the quay of the Danube, laughing and singing. We had the empty champagne bottles with us, and we smashed them against the benches. We didn't know then, of course, that ours would be the last class in the history of the Jewish *gymnasium* in Budapest to celebrate our graduation in such a carefree way.

When I look back on the summer that followed, I think of it, in a way, as the end of my youth. As a kind of graduation present, my mother took me on a tour to visit her relatives in Nagyvárad. Today the name of the city is Oradea Mare, because it is now part of Rumania. But that summer of 1943 Nagyvárad was still very Hungarian, and the Jews who lived there—at least the ones I knew—had a marvelous life. The Jewish business people lived in Hollywood-style villas with swimming pools and tennis courts. We stayed with my Uncle Feri Ullmann, the husband of my mother's sister Csilla. Csilla had died under tragic circumstances, but we were still on good terms with Uncle Feri (who had remarried), and I had a fabulous time with my cousin, his daughter Luci. There seemed to be no end of parties and festivities. I remember meeting a young man there who was studying music; he wanted to become a symphony orchestra conductor. His name was Laci Roth. Years later I heard that he survived the concentration camps because of his musical talent. Some of the Nazi big shots in those camps were music lovers and gave special privileges and protection to inmates who were musicians.

Uncle Feri and Luci and all that part of the family were not so lucky. They perished in one of the death camps. The summer of 1943 was the last summer I shared with them.

From Nagyvárad Mother took me to Siofok, on Lake Balaton. This was a beautiful summer resort where lots of Hungarian Jews came for their vacation. In fact, some anti-Semites called Siofok "Zsido-fok"; *zsido* means "Jewish." We spent a few weeks there. Pista Reiss turned up there too, and we had nice times together, boating, swimming, and dancing.

I don't know whether Pista was the sort of man my parents would have picked for me under normal circumstances. The age difference didn't matter all that much to them: my father was sixteen years older than my mother when they married. But Pista's background wasn't anything like mine. He was a self-made man. His father died when he was three. He had an older sister, Klári. The mother was unable to care for both her children, so she kept Klári but put Pista into an orphanage. When I met Pista, he was already in business for himself. He learned the textile business at Ujpesti Textiles, one of the biggest factories in the line in Hungary. The owner of Ujpesti was Mr. Ágoston, who was to become a very dear friend of ours. After a while Pista left Ágoston and opened up his own business, with a gentile partner, Mr. Györi, making goosedown comforters. This was a very good business because in those days of high fuel costs everybody in Europe used comforters. The comforters were made of silks and brocades, and most of the work was done by hand. It was a delicate, costly operation, and Pista's business was at a very prominent location, in the City Hall building of Budapest.

Anyway, Pista impressed everyone as charming, intelligent and successful.

On my birthday in November 1943, Pista proposed to me again. This time I said "yes."

My parents immediately started making plans for an elaborate

engagement party, a gathering for family and friends at our apartment. First of all, there was my dress. Mother took me to her
dressmaker and ordered a beautiful dress for me. It was high style
—a figure-hugging jersey material. The color was very fashionable at the time; it was called "chow-chow," like the fur of a little
Chihuahua dog, a sort of burned toast.

The party was beautiful—a kind of open house for relatives,
friends, and a few who hadn't even been invited. I received some
fantastic gifts. My cousins Zoltan, Bandi, and Eva Weiss came all
the way from Nyiregyháza—a train trip of five or six hours. My
grandfather Zucker, of course, was there, too. He was eighty
years old. I have a suspicion that at first he didn't entirely approve
of Pista because Pista was not an observant Jew and hadn't had
much of a Jewish religious education. But Pista promised he
wouldn't interfere with my keeping the laws and customs I'd
learned at my parents' home. He even took a rabbi who came
every day to teach him the rudiments of Judaism. For this reason,
and because he appreciated Pista's human qualities—above all, he
was very good to his mother—Grandfather accepted him as a
member of the family.

After the party, Pista and I had our own private celebration.
He took me to the Parisienne Grille, a high-class night club on
Margit Sziget, an island in the middle of the Danube from which
you got a magnificent view of the Budapest skyline. My world
and the world of my parents was changing. Under normal circumstances, my father would never have permitted me to go to
a night club unchaperoned with a young man, not even if it was
my fiancé. But now my parents didn't object to my going to the
Parisienne Grill alone with Pista.

We planned our wedding for March 1944. My mother and I
began to gather my trousseau. Whenever we went downtown
and I saw some beautiful linen or lingerie in a show window,
we'd go into the store and order it for me. There was one gor-
geous lingerie window—all in aqua. We went inside and bought
the whole windowful for my trousseau.

A few weeks before the date set for my wedding, Mother
collapsed. The doctors didn't really know what was the matter

with her. It was a kind of depression, very much out of character with her lively, energetic personality. We took her to a resort on Svábhegy, in the Buda mountains, where the air was good and the atmosphere relaxing. She was there for two weeks. Meanwhile, we postponed the wedding because, with Mother out of action, we couldn't proceed. When Mother felt better, we aimed for a later date. By that time another consideration entered into our planning: Pista was in a labor camp, but he escaped the worst hardships by spending time at hospitals. Eventually, he was transferred to a camp very close to Budapest, from which he was often able to get furloughs. Pista knew how to handle the authorities, and so, during our engagement, and later, too, he managed it so that he was practically commuting between the labor camp and Budapest. Meanwhile, his gentile partner, Mr. Györi, continued running the comforter business. Mr. Györi was now registered as the official owner of the business, but in reality he was acting only as a "straw man," a front for Pista.

EVA

Marianne became engaged in late fall of 1943. My whole family was there. It was a big affair, a family dinner; we came to Budapest from Nyiregyháza to attend.

My brothers were there, my parents, and, of course my grandfather, who lived in Budapest. I had the impression, from the mood and from the affair, that somehow the reality of the times was evading them.

II
Awakening

Veesenmayer's second report, scarcely one month after Marianne's engagement, contended that "the Jews are enemy number one, and the 1.1 million Jews amount to saboteurs—and they will have to be looked upon as Bolshevik vanguards." Prominent Jews were members of, or peripheral to, a Jewish Council: Men such as Kasztner, Brand, Petö, Komoly, Stern, Bandoczi, Stöckler, Boda, Krausz, and others. This council was regarded as leadership for the Jewish population of Budapest.

Ample warnings of impending doom, once a rumor or a trickle of information, was now swamping this Jewish leadership. The atrocity at Bor (where 3,700 Hungarian Jews working in a labor brigade were machine-gunned in a single act) was common knowledge, and escaped Bruce Teicholz warned leadership in April 1943, of the Polish extermination camps.

The Warsaw Ghetto revolt had erupted during Passover of 1943. What were the Council's plans? Would they measure up to the awesome responsibility of one million lives?

The Russians were moving westward. The German high command knew that the hills of Budapest were the last bastion of defence for Germany from the Russians, and that Horthy had negotiated surrender to the Russians. On March 17, 1944, Hitler sent for Horthy. There was a second meeting at Schloss Klessheim. Hitler accused Horthy's Magyars of traitorism and delayed his return by staging a fake air raid. Occupation of Hungary by Germany was imminent.

MARIANNE

The world of my girlhood ended suddenly on March 19, 1944, less than three weeks before my wedding day. It was a beautiful Sunday morning and I had a date to meet Pista on the Corso. The Corso was Budapest's famous riverside promenade on the banks of the Danube; all the elegant hotels and cafes were there, and you could stroll up and down, relax on a bench, or sit in an outdoor cafe and enjoy the scene, the flowers and the fresh spring air.

A few months earlier, Pista had taken an apartment on the Buda side of the Danube. The building was ultra-modern. The apartment was small, with a balcony. Pista and I had bought the furniture together; some of it was what they called "Swedish modern" then, and some was what we'd call Italian Provincial today. We'd chosen fine wallpaper and handsome Oriental rugs. The apartment was just the right size for a newly-married couple. I looked forward to moving with Pista into our own home.

But just as I was getting dressed for my date with Pista—I was about to put on my new spring outfit—the phone rang. It was Pista, calling me from the apartment in Buda. "Don't go out of your house," he said. "The Germans . . . I'm looking out the window and I can see the German army marching across the bridges."

I hung up the phone and turned on the radio. The news announcers sounded confused and frightened. And within a few hours not just the Buda section but the entire city of Budapest was occupied by the Germans. What we thought would never happen to us in Budapest was starting to happen on that Sunday in March 1944.

I followed Pista's advice and stayed home with my parents. Later I heard that friends of mine, young people from our set, did go out into the street. But all they could see was soldiers, German soldiers, pouring across the Danube River bridges into the city of Budapest. Not one shot was fired. No one tried to resist the Germans. But I must say that neither were these Hungarians in the streets yelling "Heil Hitler!"

After that, each day brought its own history. Posters were put up, announcements came over radios and public loudspeakers, and it seemed that new laws against Jews were made every hour on the hour.

Of course we'd heard reports about what Hitler had been doing to the Jews in the countries occupied by the Germans. We knew about arrests and deportations of Jews in those countries. But somehow we'd never quite believed that such things could happen also to us, the Jews in Hungary.

I'm not saying that before the days of Hitler, the Jews in Hungary lived in complete freedom. For one thing, there were "Jewish quotas" at the Hungarian universities. These quotas were well known and officially enforced. It didn't occur to any Jews in Hungary to protest against them. You just lived with the realities. If you were turned down by, say, the school of chemistry at the University of Budapest because the Jewish quota was already filled, you simply tried to get into another school at the same university, say, the school of economics, where they still let in Jews because the quota hadn't been filled yet that term. The following year you could try for a transfer to the school you really wanted. You could always get around such things. But what we were faced with now was clearly something new, different and terrible.

I remember that after Hitler's army marched into Budapest, all the young Jewish people in town seemed to be getting married. People wanted to belong to each other, to be together and share whatever there was still left of life. Also, there were all kinds of rumors—for instance, that if you were married, you wouldn't be deported, or at least not without your husband or wife.

I think I was one of the very few girls my age—only a teenager who'd become engaged before the Germans came and who would have got married even if everything would have remained normal.

On April 1, 1944, we received word from Pista that he had arranged for a few days' furlough from his labor camp.

On April 4, Pista came to my parents' apartment to pick me up for our civil marriage ceremony, at City Hall. In Hungary, you had to have a civil ceremony first, only after that were you permitted to marry in a religious ceremony, Christian or Jewish, in addition—if you cared to do that.

The date set for our religious ceremony was April 6. We planned to have the wedding at the big Orthodox synagogue on Kazinczy Street. But that very morning, at the last minute, we learned that the synagogue had been closed. So we understood that we'd have to have the ceremony at home, at my parents' apartment. We found a big prayer shawl that could be held over us in place of a regular bridal canopy. Then we asked a gentile friend who lived on the top floor of my parents' apartment building whether we could use her balcony for the ceremony, so that it could be held directly under the open sky. In Hungary, this was the strict Orthodox tradition; even if we had married at the synagogue, the ceremony would not have been in the sanctuary but in the courtyard. Our gentile friend, who happened to be a photographer, asked me whether I would like her to take pictures of my wedding. But I said, "No, thank you. This is one occasion I'd rather remember in my head than from wedding pictures." I thought I'd look ridiculous in my wedding outfit—a short white shantung suit from the summer before with the long veil of Brussels lace that all the brides in my mother's family had worn at their weddings. Mother had bought me a traditional white bridal gown, but we'd lent it to a gentile woman, and she didn't want to return it to us. Perhaps she'd sold it—who knows? We just knew that this was no time for Jews to claim their property from gentiles.

I still remember the traditional pre-wedding ceremony of going to the *mikvah*—the ritual bath. Married Jewish women—if they're observant—go to the *mikvah* each month after their period. Brides go before the wedding so that they may come to their bridegrooms in a spirit of purity. My mother escorted me to the *mikvah*. The *mikvah* of Budapest's Orthodox Jewish community was a rather sophisticated affair. The Budapest *mikvah* gave you a choice of second class or first class, depending on the fee you wanted to pay. In first class you had a private dressing room and a complete beauty salon—hair dryer, and so forth—for afterwards.

I can even remember the dress my mother wore for my wedding. It certainly wasn't the kind of gown she'd planned to put on for the wedding of her only child. I remember how she climbed a chair, reached into the top shelf of her closet to take out one of her hats, and just slapped it on top of her head. It was as if she said to herself, "My God, this certainly isn't the wedding I imagined for my only child!"

Marianne, 1943

three cousins at the beach: Luci Ullman, Eva Weisz and Marianne Lowy 1932

Steven Reiss boarding Pam Am clipper for Australia, July 1947

Marianne Reiss, 1974

Eva and Victor Aitay (1948, Pittsburgh)

Victor Aitay (1959, Chicago Symphony)

Klári, Tomas, Zsuzsi and Tibor
Vayda (Budapest, 1949)

Marianne and Tibor Waldman
(Lake Hopatcong, about 1960)

Hilda, Henrick, and Charles
Zucker (Dec. 1946, Budapest)

Mrs. Adolph Zukor with her niece Marianne

Eva and Martin Korda, 1947

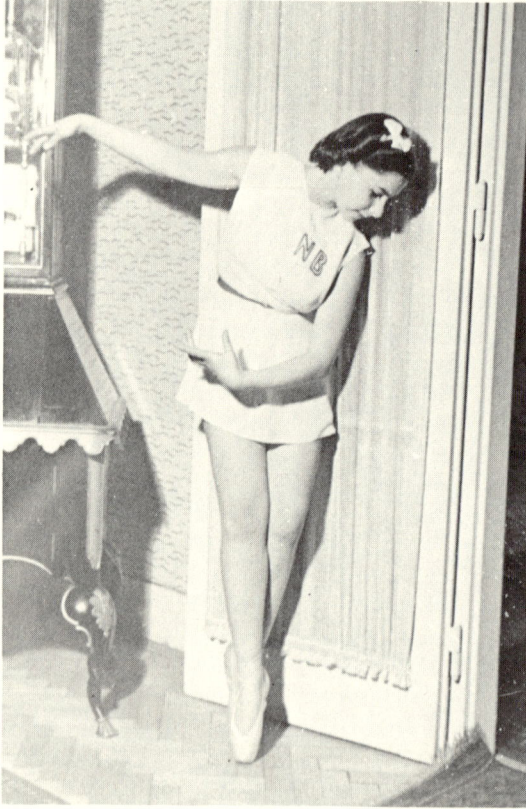

Marianne, age 14, at home

ARANKA

After I had put on my own dress and hat, I helped my daughter into her wedding clothes. I took from the closet a little white silk suit she had from the summer before, and the veil of Brussels lace that I had from my own mother. I pinned that veil on Marianne's head, stepped back and looked at her. I said to her, "My darling, this wasn't the way I planned your wedding outfit, but this is the way you'll have to get married. There's nothing I can do about it." My son-in-law was anxious to get married because he thought that perhaps our whole family could be saved in that way.

So Marianne and Pista were married on the balcony of a very nice gentile family on the top floor of our apartment building. They were married by Rabbi Steiff, who was then the Orthodox chief rabbi of Budapest. I sent somebody to pick up my father and his wife so they could come to my daughter's wedding. My daughter's wedding day was the day on which the Jews in Budapest had been ordered to put on the yellow Star of David. After the ceremony the bride and groom left us to go to their new apartment on the other side of town. I wanted to be with my daughter as long as possible, so my husband and I went with the young couple as far as the bus station. And I looked up to heaven and said, "*Mein Gott*, this is the first day Jews have to wear a yellow star and my daughter is leaving us." It was a terrible day.

MARIANNE

The only new part of my bridal outfit was a pair of white gloves.
I thought that white gloves would make my dress a little more
formal, to go with my grandmother's veil. So I sent my best
friend out to try to get me a pair. My friend Ervin ran all over
town and finally came up with a pair of new white gloves!

I don't remember what my bridegroom wore, but it must have
been a nice suit because Pista was always very clothes-conscious.
I do remember the outfit of his niece—Zsuzsi, the daughter of his
sister Klári Vayda. Zsuzsi was just five years old, and she had on
a lovely spring dress, with little shiny black patent leather shoes.
I think she was the only one at the wedding with a genuine smile
on her face. She came to the wedding with her mother and her
father, Tibor Vayda. Of course, her grandmother, Pista's mother,
was also there. My own cousin, Zoltan Weiss, was one of the four
young men that held the prayer shawl over Pista and me as a
bridal canopy. Aside from the rabbi, the only people outside the
family we invited were my best girlfriend, my very good friend
Ervin from across the street, and a young man who was the son
of a friend of my mother's.

The ceremony on that rooftop balcony was in the strict Hungarian Orthodox Jewish tradition. I was marched seven times
around my bridegroom. I think I was in a daze while I performed
in that part of our wedding, because all I remember is that everybody around me was crying. And those were not tears of happiness.

After the ceremony, my mother served a wedding luncheon at the apartment. She wanted to have chicken soup, the traditional "golden soup" that is supposed to symbolize a good life for the bride and groom. There was still a kosher restaurant open in our neighborhood, so we sent someone there to see whether they had some chicken soup. But all they could come up with was a kind of horrible, muddy-looking bean soup.

I don't remember what the rest of the meal was like, except that in the middle of it all the air raid sirens went off. I think this was the first Allied air raid on Budapest. At any rate, we left all the food on the table and ran down to the air raid shelter. This was great fun for my new niece, Zsuzsi—the sirens, the running, the people and the tumult. It was all very exciting for her. For us grown-ups, it was more upsetting than anything else.

When the all-clear sounded we went back to the apartment to finish our meal. While we were eating, the doorbell rang. It was a young man who we thought had already left Hungary. He told us that although he had all his papers together, including a permit to enter a neutral country, he wouldn't be able to leave Hungary after all, because the Hungarian authorities weren't issuing exit visas any more. A sad note on which to end a wedding celebration!

After the guests had left, my mother helped me pack for the move to my new apartment. My parents went with Pista and me as far as the bus station. Lujza, our former maid, was also there to help, carrying my belongings and some food. My going-away outfit included a raincoat of a fancy material known as "balloon silk;" the latest Hungarian fashion—with the yellow Star of David sewn onto it in accordance with the latest German orders. As I walked out of my parents' apartment building, I took off the raincoat. I never put it on again except when I entered a house where I was known as a Jew.

Pista and I spent almost all of our wedding night in the air raid shelter of our new home.

Pista still had his very convenient "arrangement" with the labor camp authorities. At five o'clock each morning the orderly who acted as his escort would pick him up to take him to the labor camp. At the end of each day the orderly brought him back to our apartment to spend the night.

While Pista was away, I did some thinking about the future. By then we realized that food and other necessities of life were getting scarce, and money would lose its value, so we went by the old tradition that gold was always the safest currency. With gold, you could buy anything. We managed to convert some of our cash into 500 gold Napoleons—one gold Napoleon was worth 20 French francs. The problem was where to hide these coins so we could have them available whenever we would need them. Well, in one corner of our apartment we had a huge pot in which we grew a rubber plant. So I buried the Napoleons in that pot, and each time I needed to buy something, I'd take out one of the Napoleons and exchange it for the goods we wanted. I must say that was an ingenious way of supplying ourselves with whatever we needed.

The Passover holiday was approaching, and Pista and I made plans to spend it at my parents' home. It was early in the morning of Passover eve when I arrived at my parents' apartment. My parents were still asleep, so I let myself in without awakening them. Then the doorbell rang. I went to open the door. There stood two men in civilian clothes; they produced official papers identifying them as coming from the police. They said they were looking for Endre Lowy. When I asked what they wanted from my father, they answered that they had orders to interrogate him. Usually, when such things happened, the accused was charged with listening to broadcasts from Allied countries. On the books, listening to enemy broadcasts was a crime punishable by death. And it was very easy for anyone to be charged with that offense because almost everybody was listening to the British radio. In our family, we listened to the foreign radio, which began each broadcast with the "Dah-dah-dah-*daaah*" motif from Beethoven's Fifth Symphony. "Dot-dot-dot-dash" is the Morse code for V, and V stood for victory against Hitler.

My mother came out from the bedroom in her negligee and wanted to know what was going on. Then, of course, my father appeared also. The two plainclothesmen asked him all kinds of silly questions but of course they weren't really interested in his answers. They told him to get dressed and pack up underwear for a day or two because he was going to police headquarters for questioning.

My mother got down on her knees and begged the men not to take her husband away. She held onto the coat of one of the plainclothesmen, trying to hold him back, but it didn't help. The men said that if my father hadn't done anything, he'd be released after the interrogation. If not, we'd be notified where he was so we'd be able to see him or bring him anything he needed.

My father did not come home; they imprisoned him. My husband Pista said we'd better take some active steps to save ourselves. You never knew who'd be next. So he went out to get new Aryan documents for members of his family and mine. Also, he tried to find gentiles who would give us shelter in their homes in case the Germans started mass arrests of Jews. Pista had a former girlfriend, a Catholic. I thought of her as an older woman, compared to me, at least. I was only eighteen and she was probably in her early thirties. This woman had some other Jewish ex-boyfriends, too. One of these men had a beautiful villa in one of the newer suburbs of Budapest. But he was no longer there; I was told he was in a labor camp, or maybe, by that time, he'd already been sent to a concentration camp. Anyway, the gentile lady had moved into that man's villa and lived there all by herself. She offered my husband to take me in and get me Aryan papers making me out to be her sister, who'd come from the provinces to live with her. The idea didn't appeal to me much, but I did as Pista told me. I took my belongings, and moved in with his ex-girlfriend and Pista had to go back to labor camp. From time to time he'd come to visit me for a couple of hours, but mostly I was left by myself because my landlady went to work every morning.

We entrusted that woman with some of our valuable possessions, including the veil of Brussels lace in which I had been married, some furs, most of my trousseau, and a lot of silver and other family treasures. We never saw any of these things again. Apparently, she thought she should have some reward for saving me from the Germans.

The villa was beautiful, in a lovely garden suburb, far away from other houses. It was a rather lonely place, but that didn't matter as long as I had a chance of escaping the Germans.

However, it seemed the gendarmes had their eyes on that house. Perhaps the Jewish man who owned it had been a prominent businessman and the police wondered what was going on in the house when the Jew who used to live in it was supposed to be away in a concentration camp.

Anyway, a few days after I moved in, the doorbell rang. I was by myself because my landlady had already gone to work. I opened the door. Four or five gendarmes were standing in the doorway. They came inside and asked me who I was, and who else was living in the house. I told them that, for the moment, I was there all alone, and I showed them my documents certifying that I was a pureblooded Aryan.

I remember there was a beautiful big dining room with a huge, solid, oval-shaped mahagony table. The gendarmes led me into that room and sat down around that table. Then they began to question me. First, they just asked general questions, but then the questions became more specific. It was a kind of cross-examination about the Catholic religion and its customs, including such prayers as the Hail Mary. The idea was to find out whether I really was a Christian; as my papers said.

This questioning seemed to last an eternity, but actually I don't think it took more than an hour or so. I'd picked up many facts about the Catholic religion from our maid Lujza, who'd been a very faithful member of the Church, and so I managed to give those gendarmes all the right answers. They wagged their heads at each other, exchanged whispers and finally left the house. But their parting words were, "We'll be back."

I wasn't going to wait for the gendarmes to come back. I sent a message to my family in town that I was coming home, and so, after just about a week in that fancy hideout, I returned to Budapest.

EVA

After our farm was looted in the fall of 1938, my parents, my brother Bandi, and I fled to Budapest. From there, we went to Nyiregyháza. I remained at home with my parents and studied such practical skills as fashion design, sewing, and doll-making. It was wise in those times to learn a trade with which you could make a living.

On March 19, 1944, the day the Germans took Budapest, they also occupied Nyiregyháza. But it took a few weeks before they turned their attention to the Jews in Nyiregyháza and other big cities. They started with the Jews in the little villages, arresting them and bringing them into the larger towns and cities, where ghettoes had been set up for them.

I couldn't go to my cousin Marianne's wedding in Budapest because Jews weren't allowed to travel from one city to another anymore.

My brother Zoltan was at the wedding, because he was then living in Budapest. He had taken "unofficial" leave from labor camp but managed to keep from being found and arrested. As a matter of fact, he was still operating his textile factory. Now Zoltan knew a gentile woman, a dancer, who liked to help and was not afraid of adventure. This woman said she'd try to help him save his family. She agreed to hide me for a while in her own apartment in Budapest. So Zoltan sent her to pick me up in Nyiregyháza, with a set of Aryan papers and to take me to Budapest by train. She did this, but she couldn't do anything for my parents anymore, because the very next day my father and mother were evicted from our home and taken to the ghetto of Nyiregyháza.

In Budapest, I spent no more than one week at the apartment of Zoltan's gentile friend. The people in the building saw me in the air raid shelter and the rumor went around that I was Jewish. Zoltan's friend explained that I was a relative of hers who had come to visit her from out of town, but that didn't help. Unlike my cousin Marianne, I definitely look Jewish. So my "hostess" suggested that I find another place to live. My aunt Aranka Lowy, my mother's sister, took me into her apartment. I'll never forget what she did for me, away from my parents for the first time.

ZOLTAN

By 1943 things had become pretty bad at my textile mill on the
outskirts of Budapest because it was virtually impossible for Jew-
ish-owned textile businesses to get yarn and raw material. So my
partner Imre Bodonyi and I looked for a gentile to become part
owner of our place; it was the one chance for our business to
survive. Eventually we found such a man. He was Ervin Stojkovitz, a Hungarian of Slavic origin. Before the war, he'd worked
in Germany and made some good business connections there.
Now he wanted to be an independent businessman and the idea
of becoming a partner in Jewish firm—on easy financial terms
because the Jews would need him—appealed to him. So, both
sides got what they wanted. Stojkovitz had a business of his own,
with about 25 employees, and Imre and I had a chance of surviving economically. Things became better for us almost as soon as
Stojkovitz came in with us; he got us a big order for German
army uniforms.

Each day, I commuted by train between Budapest, where I had
my apartment, and the place outside the city where the plant was
located. And so things remained fairly tolerable until March 1944.

On March 20, 1944, the day after the Germans entered Budapest, the commuters' train on which I was returning to the city
from my factory was stopped at the Eastern Railroad Terminal.
All the passengers were ordered to get off and show their identification papers. The Jews were told to line up on one side, separate

from the gentiles. Then all of us Jews were shoved into large police vans and driven straight to police headquarters. After some questioning we were told to get back into the police vans, and back we went to the railroad station. There, we were put aboard a train without being told where we were going. After a trip of several hours we arrived at the town of Kistarcsa. In that town there was an internment camp for enemy aliens. Now the camp was used also for Jews. There must have been thousands of Jews in that camp—old people, men, women, and children. And it seemed that the camp wasn't prepared for such a mass of people. There was almost no food—and not much else either—until the Jewish community of the town began to organize things a little. After a couple of days the community sent us food and cooking facilities; this made things slightly more bearable.

About two weeks later, to my biggest surprise, two other men and I were summoned to General Veesenmeyer, the big-shot SS officer who was in charge of the camp. Veesenmeyer handed each of us a slip of paper and told us we were free and could go home. Soon enough I found out who had saved me. When my partner Imre Bodonyi learned that I'd been arrested, he notified Stojko-vitz immediately, and Stojkovitz, with his good German connec-tions, was able to get me out. He received a very nice compensa-tion for his troubles. My parents in Nyiregyháza turned over to him a big bundle of securities. Under the new laws, Jews were supposed to deposit all their stocks and certificates with the au-thorities, but my father, instead of doing that, gave the stocks to Stojkovitz as a gift.

I returned to my small apartment in Budapest, which wasn't far from my Aunt Aranka's apartment on Akacfa 6. I still remem-ber that first Passover in Budapest under German occupation. My parents, my brother Bandi and my sister were in Nyiregyháza, but Jews couldn't travel from one city to another anymore, so I had to spend the holiday in Budapest. My aunt Aranka's husband had just been arrested, and everything was pretty upset. I cele-brated the Passover *seder* at the apartment of my grandfather Henrick Zucker and his wife, Hilda. Grandfather's other two guests were a man and his daughter who'd escaped to Budapest from Poland. We had just finished chanting the *kiddush*, the holiday blessing over wine with which the *seder* begins, when the air raid sirens started to blow. We had to go down to the air raid shelter in the basement of the building, and there we stayed until we heard the all-clear siren at 2 A.M. Then we went back upstairs and continued our *seder*. It was the fastest, shortest *seder* I ever attended!

Meanwhile, in the provinces, they were putting the Jews into ghettoes; in the smaller places the Jews were moved into abandoned buildings, into old synagogues or abandoned factories. Then, rumors began to spread that the Jews were going to be deported to camps in Poland for the duration of the war for fear that the Jews would act as a fifth column against the Germans if the Russians tried to invade Hungary. Of course none of us could picture the mass killings of Auschwitz and the other death camps; we'd heard the rumors but we made ourselves believe that these were just atrocity stories, the kind that make the rounds during every war. We couldn't believe that such things could really happen in the twentieth century. Unfortunately, we soon got our rude awakening; the horrors were infinitely worse than we had imagined.

I was very lucky to be able to smuggle at least my sister Eva out of Nyiregyháza and bring her to Budapest. I knew a gentile woman in Budapest, and I paid her to go to Nyiregyháza and act as Eva's escort. She brought Eva a new set of Aryan documents and, as an added safeguard against being caught, a gypsy costume which she told Eva to put on for the train ride to Budapest. The woman was a dancer; that's how she was able to get her hands on such a costume. Unfortunately I was unable to save my parents and my brother Bandi. On June 6, 1944, the day the Americans first landed on the beaches of Normandy, my father, mother, and brother were deported from the Nyiregyháza ghetto to "the East." Bandi perished in Dachau early in 1945. Had he survived only a few days longer, he would have been liberated by the Allies.

In Budapest, Eva went straight to aunt Aranka's apartment. I had to give up my own apartment and move in with aunt Aranka, too, because the Germans had ordered all Jews in Budapest to move into buildings they classed as "Jewish houses." These were apartment buildings in certain sections of Budapest. Jews who'd already been living in these "Jewish houses" all along could stay in their apartments, but the Jews who moved into these houses weren't allowed to take apartments of their own, not even if there were vacancies. They had to move into the apartments of Jewish tenants who were already living in the building. Fortunately, Aunt Aranka's apartment building was designated as a "Jewish house," so the Lowys were able to stay put. (Uncle Endre eventually was released because of the Swedish papers he was able to get.) Eva and I moved in with Uncle Endre and Aunt Aranka; so did friends of the family, Willy and Ethel Grosz, along with another lady. Somehow all of these people managed to fit into that one apartment. The neighborhood in which Aranka's building and the other "Jewish houses" were located eventually became the ghetto of Budapest.

With Eichmann present, one day after occupation a Jewish Council was ordered formed to exercise jurisdiction over all Jews. Samu Stern was elected President. A few days later there was an American air raid. Eichmann demanded and received from the Council 500 apartments as damages. The next day the yellow star was ordered worn by Jews. The day after that (April 6, 1944) Marianne was married.

Thereafter a deluge of edicts and orders against the Jews were issued. A new Council was organized. This Council, eventually was effectively in control of two voices: Rezsö Kasztner and Jöel Brand. The Council bypassed the Horthy regime who were still in effective control and rushed to deal with the Germans. Both Kasztner and Brand survived. Brand's "trucks for blood" deal (a failure), and Kasztner's "transport" and many dealings with the Germans are a matter of record.

EVA

I stayed at the apartment of my aunt Aranka Lowy from the end of April 1944, until the middle of October that year. I did not use my Aryan documents to go "underground" but lived openly as a Jew in a "Jewish house."

Early in June 1944, I was married to András Perkedi. The Perkedis had been gentleman farmers near Nyiregyháza, just like my own family. The wedding took place in Budapest, at the apartment of my aunt Aranka, just as her daughter Marianne had got married there in the spring. Of course my parents couldn't attend, because Jews were forbidden to travel between cities, but I was able to phone my parents long distance and tell them I was getting married. My parents still had a phone because my father was a privileged person; he was a member of the *Judenrat* in the ghetto of Nyiregyháza. That was the Jewish Council set up by the Germans to act as intermediaries between the Jews in the ghetto and the German authorities. Most of the *Judenrat* people in the ghettos were decent, upright individuals, who'd been picked for the job because they had been known as leaders of the Jewish community before the war, and many of them became real martyrs, singled out for special mistreatment. My own parents were deported on June 6, 1944 two days before the day the Allies landed in France, and were killed in Auschwitz.

The only member of my immediate family present at my wedding was my brother Zoltan. *

Soon after András had to go back to his camp, a few kilometers from Budapest. I never saw my husband again. In October 1944, he came back to Budapest to look for my brother Zoltan and me; he wanted to get new Aryan documents to us so we could save ourselves. But he couldn't find us because, a few days before that, we'd all gone into hiding. András was caught in the street and, as we later learned, taken to Buchenwald. After the war I placed search ads in newspapers requesting information on he whereabouts of András Perkedi. I received several answers from survivors who said they'd last seen him in Buchenwald. But nobody knew how he had died. Years later, when I became interested in remarrying, I was told that even though it was obvious by then that András couldn't have survived, I couldn't get married again under Jewish law unless I could produce acceptable evidence about when and how András had died. Then I found out that the German records of Buchenwald had been saved. The Germans had been very precise about record-keeping in the camps; and so, when I had someone look through the record books, András' name was there, together with the information that he had been shot in Buchenwald at end of February 1945.

KLÁRI REISS VAYDA

Klári Reiss Vayda, now in her sixties, is the older sister of Marianne's first husband, Pista Reiss, and the mother of Zsuzsi, who was the youngest guest at Marianne's marriage to Pista. Klári and her husband, Tibor, also have a son, Tomas, who was born after the war. Klári, her husband, and the two children remained in Hungary after the war, leaving the country only after the Revolution of 1956. The Vaydas settled in Los Angeles, where Zsuzsi (now Mrs. Sobel) acted in movie roles under the name of Valerie Varda and where Tomas is now a professor of mathematics.

At the time when all the Jews in Budapest were ordered to move into the "Jewish houses," my husband, Tibor Vayda, was in a labor camp near Budapest. Later, he was transferred to a labor camp in Kolomea, Poland, where he was wounded in the shoulder. Meanwhile, I looked for places where the rest of my family might be safe from arrest. I turned to a gentile named Németi, a bachelor who was friendly with Pista's business partner. Mr. Németi was a high-ranking officer in the Hungarian army; he had been decorated several times for bravery. This Mr. Németi helped my brother Pista Reiss obtain Aryan papers for me, for my own dear mother, and for my mother-in-law, and allowed the three of us to move into his summer home in a village far away from Budapest. That area was famous for its spas and vineyards.

According to my forged Aryan documents, I was Mr. Németi's wife, and the two mothers were his mother, and mother-in-law, respectively. Mr. Németi came to visit us every two or three weeks on furlough, while we three women were "spending our vacation" at "our" summer home. The neighbors all respected Mr. Németi tremendously and were happy that he'd finally got married. "Such a fine young couple," they said. "What a pity Mr. Németi has to be stationed so far away from his bride."

My daughter Zsuzsi, who was not yet six years old, was staying in another village with her aunt Gizi, Tibor's sister-in-law. Gizi was a gentile and passed Zsuzsi off as her daughter. Years later, in America, Zsuzsi had a role in a movie with Jimmy Stewart. But she was the perfect actress already when she was five. Never once did she fall out of her role; never once did she call her Aunt Gizi anything but *anyu*—Mommy. Each morning, Zsuzsi would go out with a little basket on her arm and collect stray kittens. She was a very warm, lovely child, and I almost perished with longing for her. But I couldn't take her to the village where her two grandmothers and I were staying; it would have made the neighbors suspicious. After all, I was supposed to be only a recent bride!

As it was, I lived in constant fear that we might be exposed. One day, when I went to the baker's for bread, a miserable gentile youth, who wanted to flirt with me, started questioning me about the place where my Aryan papers said I'd been born. It seemed this was the same place that he came from, and I knew almost nothing about it. I had a difficult time getting away from him.

Finally, I told Mr. Németi that I couldn't stand this uncertainty any longer. I was sure that one of us—either one of the two mothers or I—would eventually slip somewhere and that would be the end of all of us. I said I'd much rather go back to Budapest where I could be near the wife and family of my brother Pista.

So, one day late in August or early September 1944, my "husband," Mr. Németi, looking very distinguished in his officer's uniform and medals, came to the village to fetch my mother, my mother-in-law, and me. We then picked up Zsuzsi from my sister-in-law's summer home, and boarded a train back to Budapest. Naturally, Mr. Németi didn't do all this out of pure unselfishness. My dear brother Pista paid him a fortune for his help and for the two or three months that we stayed at his villa. Of course there is no denying that Németi put himself in grave danger by getting involved with us. And because of his high position in the army, the risk for him was all the greater.

In Budapest we couldn't go back to our old apartment, because our building was not one of the "Jewish houses." So we moved into the one place where they let us in—the apartment of Pista's mother-in-law, Aranka Lowy.

All this time, my husband, Tibor, had been in labor camps. Then, after he was shot in Kolomea, he was fortunate enough to be brought back to Budapest, where he was placed into an army hospital. That's how he survived, because later, when the Germans wanted to move all the wounded in that hospital to Germany, Tibor managed to go AWOL—thanks in large measure to that wonderful Swedish humanitarian, Raoul Wallenberg.

TIBOR VAYDA

Tibor Vayda, husband of Klári Reiss Vayda, was in the book business in Hungary. In Los Angeles, he was active as an art dealer until his recent retirement.

I come from a nice Jewish family, not Orthodox but a good Jewish family. We were seven children. I am the youngest, and what's very, very unusual about us is that my entire family went through the war right there in Hungary—and survived. Every one of us was in a different place. Three of my brothers were married to Christian women, who saved them from being put in a concentration camp. I have two sisters. One of them was hidden by one of our gentile sisters-in-law.

I did my compulsory service in the regular Hungarian army for about two years—from 1937 until 1940, I believe. After that, Jews were no longer allowed to be in the regular army. They were transferred to labor camps. I myself spent four years at various labor camps.

In 1944, I was injured at the labor camp in Poland. They put me on a hospital train that was taking wounded soldiers to Hungary. I was able to walk, so I could have escaped from the train, but I didn't want to do that because I wanted to get to Budapest and find out what happened to my family. In Budapest they put all of us into a school that had been converted into a hospital. After about three days I was able to get hold of Pista's family on the telephone. The next day, my wife, Klári, came to visit me. She was looking very pretty and said she had news for me. We just became Swedish citizens, she told me. She and I now had Swedish *Schutzpässe,* Swedish passports.

MARIANNE

All through the summer and early fall of 1944, my parents' household in Budapest kept on growing. Mother took into the apartment about half a dozen people who'd been displaced from their
homes by the German law that Jews could live only in "Jewish
houses." This included me, because my apartment was in a non-
Jewish neighborhood. My parents' apartment building was just
at the border of the area of "Jewish houses" that eventually became the ghetto of Budapest. In addition to my parents and
myself—Pista was mostly away from home, in a labor camp—
there now were in the apartment my cousins Eva and Zoltan
Weisz, Pista's sister Klári Vayda, her daughter Zsuzsi, and our
friends Willy and Ethel Grosz, along with the Gross' Jewish
live-in maid.

When Zoltan's lady friend offered to escort Eva from
Nyiregyháza to Budapest, we sent a message to my aunt Rozsi
and her husband Musu—the parents of Zoltan and Eva—that
they should also try to get out of Nyiregyháza and travel to
Budapest, with faked Aryan papers, or whatever. But Uncle
Musu, who was in the *Judenrat*, insisted that he, of all people,
couldn't do anything to violate the law because it might endanger
the lives of the Jews who would have to stay behind in
Nyiregyháza. And so the Weisz' stayed in the Nyiregyháza
ghetto, and that's how they eventually were deported from there
to Auschwitz on June 6, 1944.

During that summer, it became known in Budapest that the Swedish government was trying to do certain things to save the Jews in Hungary. They were giving out Swedish *Schutzpässe*, safe-conduct papers that placed Jews under the protection of the Swedish consulate in Budapest. This was the work of the attaché Raoul Wallenberg. Pista was quick to find out about ways of getting these Swedish papers, because he learned that even if you were already in jail, you would be released if someone obtained Swedish papers for you. That's how my father finally got out of prison, where he had been since the day before Passover.

Actually, it wasn't a prison; it was a hotel on the Svábhegy, in the Buda mountains, that had been converted into what they called an internment camp. So my father wasn't very far away from the hotel where we'd taken my mother in the spring before my wedding to recover from her depression. We were allowed to come at certain times and bring him food. I remember going out there by commuters' train from Budapest, taking soup and vegetables for my father in a dinner pail. I would give the pail to the guard, who then gave its contents to my father and returned it to me empty. I never wore the yellow Star of David on my clothes when I made those trips. Maybe it was a little reckless of me, but I don't look Jewish and no one ever stopped me.

Meanwhile, Pista managed to get Swedish papers for my father on July 31, 1944—it was Mother's birthday—the miracle came to pass. I remember that we opened the rear door of our apartment that led to the corridor—probably to air out the apartment, which by that time was more than overcrowded. When we opened the door—I'll never forget this—and I looked down from a corridor window into the courtyard, I saw a familiar figure. It was my father! You can imagine the elation and the joy, and the scream I let out when I saw that this was really my father . . . and my mother and everybody else from the apartment came running. . . . He looked terrible; I couldn't imagine that someone could change so much in only a few months' time. He'd lost a lot of weight and his clothes were hanging from his body. But the main thing was that he's come back to us alive.

Taking care of our big household on Akacfa 6 was not easy.

But somehow, through Mrs. Grosz, who was a smart woman and knew her way around, we always had enough food. So much so that every time the doorbell rang, a bag of flour or sugar or a dozen eggs went down the toilet because we didn't know who might be at the door. These foods were rationed, and Jews weren't supposed to have any of them at all. If we'd been discovered with such staple items, not only would we have been taken off to jail—and who knows to what other place from there—but all the other tenants in our building would have been endangered. So, in order to protect ourselves and our neighbors we sometimes had to let our most precious foods go down the drain.

All the people in our building knew one another and were drawn together by the problems and the fears they shared. We, the young people, would gather together on Saturdays and sing Hebrew and other Jewish songs, led by one friend who had a beautiful voice and was in fact a professional singer.

It was in my parents' apartment that my cousin Eva Weisz was married to her first husband, András Perkedi, in June 1944. They'd been sweethearts ever since they both were fourteen. One day, András called Eva and said he'd be given a short furlough from the labor camp where he was stationed. Would she want to get married then? Of course she said yes, because she'd wanted that very much all along.

Naturally, we wanted to get the consent of Eva's parents, my Aunt Rozsi and Uncle Musu,* if possible. So we called them in Nyiregyháza, and they gave the young couple their blessing over the telephone. That was the last time we ever heard their voices.

Eva's wedding was simple and fast. The gentile people on the top floor had moved out when our building became a "Jewish house" and we didn't even think to ask the new Jewish tenants whether we could use the balcony on which Pista and I had been married. We wanted the ceremony to be an inconspicuous as possible.

Early in the fall, Pista's sister Klári, Pista's mother, and Klári's daughter Zsuzsi moved in with us. They had been in hiding in

*Mör Weisz

the countryside, with false Aryan papers, at the summer home of a gentile friend of Pista's business partner, a bachelor by the name of Németi. Németi was an officer in the Hungarian army, a handsome man. Németi agreed to let Klári, and also her mother and my mother-in-law, live at his villa, with Klári posing as the bachelor's new bride. Zsuzsi was with one of her father's gentile sisters-in-law. But after a couple of months Klári couldn't bear being separated from her little girl anymore. Also, she was afraid that she and the two old ladies would be caught posing as gentiles. So they all came back to Budapest and settled in with us, at Akacfa 6.

That summer in Budapest Jews weren't allowed to go to beaches anymore, or to other places of entertainment. So about the greatest outdoor entertainment we had was to stroll through the streets. Our main indoor entertainment, except for our Saturday singing sessions, was the Ouija board. I don't know who first brought in that new game. Later, I heard that a kind of Ouija board game was popular in the United States, too, during the early 1940s. Anyway, we'd sit around a table which had on it a board with all kinds of numerals and mysterious characters on it. On top of the board there was a glass. Everybody sitting around the table had to put his hands on the glass, and one of the players conducted a séance. The idea was that the warmth of the players' hands would make the glass move slowly over the board. The symbols over which it stopped were supposed to give you answers to any questions you had about the present or the future. Whether or not you really believed in the mystic powers of the Ouija board didn't count. The main thing was that we had a form of entertainment, and all kinds of optimistic hopes for the future were raised by the questions we asked the Ouija board, and the answers we received.

After June 6, when the Allies landed in France, air raids on Budapest came more and more often. The air raids didn't make us unhappy. We told ourselves that if we got hit by a bomb, we'd never know it, so what was the difference? On the other hand, if the bomb missed us, it meant we'd get one day closer to the time when we'd be liberated. That was our one pleasure from the bombings. The other pleasure we got was that the gentiles were getting a kind of poetic justice. They didn't allow us to go to the public swimming pools, or on picnics and excursions. Well, now they couldn't go either; they had to spend their Sundays running to the air-raid shelters and waiting for the all-clear.

We young people had a kind of "underground" organization. There were in Budapest certain young Jewish boys and girls who had come to town from the countryside. They traveled with forged Aryan papers and passed as gentiles. We, who were living as Jews in the "Jewish houses," would get together with these out-of-towners at various places. We called it a *buli* in Hungarian —an "arrangement" by which we'd meet and go on long walks. During those walks we'd exchange underground news sheets and discuss the latest Allies radio broadcasts. How far had the Allies come? Where were the Nazis? Which side was advancing? Rumors were spreading all the time. Of course, everybody wanted to believe that something good was happening on the battlefronts. It became more and more difficult to listen to the British radio, but of course, everybody kept doing it, somehow or other, because that was the only way you could get the real news. You might be able to hear only a few minutes each day. Sometimes we'd decide which one of us should listen on his radio and report to the rest of us. News traveled fast. People visited each other and went around saying, "This is what I heard," or, "That's the latest news," and they tried to piece all the scraps of reports together.

There were rumors, too, about what the Germans were planning to do with the Jews. One day the story went that all the Jews in Hungary were going to be deported to concentration camps. The next day we'd hear that the Jews would be sent away to the island of Madagascar,* in the Indian Ocean, and everybody started making jokes about wearing grass skirts.

One of my mother's friends, Margit Strauss, ordered a whole new wardrobe for herself, dresses, suits, coats and hats for every

---

*The suggestion that all Jews should be resettled in Madagascar was actually voiced in anti-Semitic circles as early as the 1920's. Later, the Nazis seriously discussed Madagascar as a place where those Jews who survived the war would be sent after the final German victory. [Ed]

season of the year, and for every kind of weather or climate. She called these clothes her "escape outfits," with which she'd be able to start out on a new life no matter where she might end up. As things turned out, Margit survived the war in Budapest. She is now living in Rome.

So, people really had a sense of humor. Between the real news and the false, and living from one day to the next, we swapped jokes and played out situation comedies that made it possible for us to go on existing.

You never knew when your turn might come. Sometimes Hungarian anti-Semites set a trap for Jews. They'd tell a Jewish person there was a job for him somewhere. They'd even pay him, in cash, or in script, or in loaves of bread, and then they'd turn him over to the Gestapo. The Jews in Hungary could never be sure where they stood. According to Hungarian law, for instance, the Jews in Budapest could not be harmed as long as they lived in their "Jewish houses." So, the Hungarian police couldn't enter such a building to drag out its tenants. But there was nothing in Hungarian law to forbid the German Gestapo from going in and rounding up the Jews for deportation. Also, a Jew could be picked up in the street and arrested at any time. By the fall of 1944, no Hungarian Jew was safe, even at home, in any way, because the Hungarian police was just as free as the Gestapo to catch Jews wherever they found them. During that period the only Jews in Budapest safe from arrest and deportation were those who could find shelter in the "Swedish houses" that were under the protection of Swedish consulates. The Swiss also gave a few passports, but no shelter that I recall.

III
Gehenna

October 16, 1944 was the date agreed upon by Horthy to surrender Hungary to the Russians. One day earlier Horthy's son Nicholas was kidnapped by the Gestapo to force the Septuagenarian Regent to resign. The Arrow-Cross (Home Guard) and Szalasi took control, and the dejewification of Budapest commenced in earnest. The provinces had been dejewified. Wallenberg had been in Budapest since July 9, but was being overwhelmed. The survival of whoever remained was now a question of chance, accident and resourcefulness.

MARIANNE

On October 15, 1944, the official Hungarian Nazi party came to power. It took as its symbol the "Arrow Cross," a cross with arrows on its corners instead of bent arms like the German swastika. Their leader, Ferenc Szálasi, attracted every type of Hungarian anti-Semite, but particularly young people. On that day, October 15, 1944, every janitor's son, or whoever felt that he'd been treated unjustly by life, put on the "Arrow Cross" armband, got a rifle, and took the law into his own hands. "Arrow Cross" gangs rampaged all over Budapest and other cities, looting and killing Jews wherever they found them.

We knew we'd have to act fast to save ourselves. We realized that the apartment on Akacfa 6 was no longer safe and that we'd have to go somewhere else, even if it meant that we couldn't stay together anymore.

By that time my cousins Eva and Zoltan had already left my parents' house and were hiding out in the suburbs at the house of Zoltan's gentile partner, Ervin Stojkovitz. Some of their childhood friends had gone with them to the same place.

One day my husband, Pista, and I packed up my parents, Pista's sister Klári and Pista's mother, and we all moved into the two rooms in the City Hall building where Pista and his gentile partner, Mr. Györi, had their place of business. By that time, because of the bombings, the business was closed. The bombers had done a good job on most of the buildings around the City Hall.

Each of us carried only a small suitcase with his most essential belongings. I carried, in addition, a little cosmetics bag where I had put my jewelry and the gold Napoleons I still had left. These were the gold coins I'd kept in the soil of my rubber plant at my apartment in Buda. When I had to leave that beautiful little apartment into which Pista and I had put so much thought and imagination, I dug out our remaining Napoleons and took them with me to my parents' apartment at Akacfa 6. Now I was taking them to a new, temporary home. I told myself that if you had gold, you could always buy the necessities of life, maybe even life itself.

And so my parents and the rest of us moved into what once had been Pista's factory. There were two rooms; the sales room in front and the workshop in the rear. We bolted the back door, and closed off the storefronts with what they called a *rolletta*, a sliding shutter. Pista's partner, Mr. Györi, assured us that we'd be safe there, at least for a few days. As long as the place remained closed in the front and in the back, it wouldn't occur to anyone that people were living inside. It would look like just another place of business that had been forced to close down by "enemy action." Mr. Györi said he'd come by each night and pass us some food through the window. There was a sink in the place, but no toilet. I think the employees of the shop had shared the toilet facilities of the store next doors. Now we used a bucket, which we covered and passed to Mr. Györi through the window each night when he came with our food.

So we spent two or three days and nights in the factory, in total darkness. We slept on the counters, covering ourselves with quilts and goosedown comforters from the workshop. Unfortunately there were lots of mice running around; they seemed to feel much more comfortable in these surroundings than we humans did. All we could do was to climb higher and higher on top of the counters and pile up our quilts and comforters in the hope that maybe the mice would get lazy and not climb all the way up to find us.

Meanwhile Pista had been able to get Swedish safe-conduct passes for everyone. I didn't really need the Swedish papers because I had forged Aryan documents. My sister-in-law Klári and my mother-in-law were the first to leave Pista's factory. Tibor's gentile sister-in-law, Gizi, came for them and escorted them through back streets and alleys to her home on the other side of town. My parents decided it would be best for them to move into one of the "Swedish houses," one of the buildings that were under the protection of the Swedish consulate. They knew that this would mean living in incredibly cramped quarters, but then they would be safe there, with their Swedish papers, under the protection of the Swedish government. Eventually Pista moved into the building of the Swedish consulate itself, where a few privileged Jews were able to find shelter. Pista was the kind of person who always knew how to deal with the authorities and how to survive, no matter what happened. My brother-in-law, Tibor, was there also.

It was decided that I, with my Aryan papers, should go into hiding at the home of our former bookkeeper, Mr. Tabák, which was safe because his wife was a gentile. The Tabák's apartment was comfortable, on a high floor. By that time, most of the gentiles in Budapest were hardly ever in their apartments anymore; they practically lived in the air-raid shelters that were in each basement and went to their apartments upstairs only to get food and other necessary supplies. The Tabák's apartment building had a very large air-raid shelter; I think it took up the entire basement of the building. So, all the tenants of the building had plenty of time and space to become acquainted. That's why Mrs. Tabák didn't want her husband to go to the air-raid shelter; she didn't want the neighbors to know that she had a Jewish husband living with her right there in the building.

If someone happened to come to the apartment, it was all right for me to be there; I didn't look Jewish. But Mr. Tabák's face was a dead giveaway. So, if I was home, it was my job, whenever the doorbell rang, to help Mr. Tabák escape from the apartment through the bathroom window. We had a special gadget made for this purpose, something like the safety belt that window cleaners put around their waist. Any time the doorbell rang, I would push him into the bathroom, help him climb on the windowsill, put the safety belt around his waist and hang him out from the bathroom window!

The Tabáks' apartment building was constructed in the old European style. The windows of the bathrooms and other inside rooms were not on the street but on an inner court with a glass roof, a kind of shaft through which a little light was let into these rooms. But it was too dark to see anything if you were standing in that inner court on ground floor level. If somebody was hanging from the bathroom window, nobody could see him. We did this trick many times, Mr. Tabák and I. When the doorbell rang, I rushed to hang him out from the bathroom window before I went back to the front to open the door. After the visitor had gone, I'd go to the bathroom to help Mr. Tabák pull himself back in again. Then I'd lock him up in the room of the apartment that had been set aside as his hideout.

I had a daily routine of my own. I would leave the Tabáks' apartment each day at noon or early in the afternoon to visit Pista at the Swedish consulate. On the way, I tried to pick up food and other necessities from the stores that were still open. One of these stores was a beautiful delicatessen shop that still had enough merchandise to make a most appealing show window. I always went into that store to buy up whatever delicacies they had that day, foods that I knew Pista and the others hiding out in the consulate could use.

After spending a couple of hours in the consulate building, I'd go back to the Tabáks' place, on foot. It was insane for a Jewish person to walk through the streets of Budapest then, but I did it. I told myself that if fate—or whatever—wanted me to be arrested or shot, it would happen no matter what precautions I took. If it was in the cards for me to live, I'd survive no matter what chances I'd take.

I also had another hangup in those days. It involved my personal possessions—my jewelry and my identification papers. For some reason I cannot explain, I felt that if I didn't carry these things on my person, or if I ever discarded any of them, I would not survive. So I carried in my handbag not only my faked Aryan papers but also, in a separate compartment, my jewelry and even my regular, legitimate Jewish identification! By that time, anybody walking through the streets of the city could be stopped by the police and asked to show his identification papers. If I'd have been caught with two sets of documents, it would have been the end. But luck was with me. I was never stopped. My family kept badgering me that it was insane to carry my jewelry around with me all the time. So, before we left, I was persuaded to put my jewelry into the safe we had built into the wall of Pista's factory. My family pointed out that in this old-fashioned, almost indestructible safe, my jewelry should survive even the worst bombings. So; much against my will, I followed my family's advice.

Meanwhile, I looked around for articles that might have barter value if the worst came to the worst. At this point, store owners were eager to sell off whatever merchandise they still had; they didn't want to be caught in a bombing with a storeful of goods. So they were willing to reduce their prices to a minimum. There was in Budapest one perfumery—you would probably call it a drugstore or pharmacy here—which had wonderful toiletry goods, but at that time, obviously very few people were interested in such things. If they were interested, they didn't dare to go out into the streets to buy them. Now this particular store knew me well because I used to buy perfumes and skin lotions from them before the war. So one day I went in and bought up their entire stock of skin lotions, hand lotions, perfumes, colognes, and other toiletries. I was able to store all this merchandise in the air raid shelter of the Tabáks' apartment building. Mrs. Tabák offered to keep it in the same corner of the shelter where she kept the cans of sardines and other foods she considered necessary for survival.

In the meantime, the air raids became worse every day, and the more bombs fell, the fewer civilians were seen in the streets. Nevertheless, I kept up my daily visits to the Swedish consulate, where Pista was. I could not go to the "Swedish house" where my parents were hidden, and I could only hope that they were safe. The threat came not only from bombs, of course, but also from the low-flying planes that machine-gunned civilians in the streets, from misfired anti-aircraft gunfire, and from the debris that fell from the bombed buildings.

Gradually, I spent most of each day at the Swedish consulate with my husband. I went back to my room in the Tabák's apartment only for the night.

Chanukah was coming and—wonder of wonders—I managed to get together some flour, shortening, nuts and other ingredients to bake holiday goodies for the Tabáks and for the people hiding in the Swedish consulate. I baked a kind of roll called *beigli;* it's made with nuts or poppy seed and is the traditional holiday pastry they serve in Hungary.

EVA

In October 1944, when the "Arrow Cross" gangs started to become active and Aunt Aranka's apartment was no longer safe, the family had to abandon the apartment and to break up. My brother Zoltan, two other girls and I found shelter, in a warehouse belonging to Zoli's factory. Gyula Adonyi and his wife, who lived and worked next door to Zoltan's factory were really good to us; they looked after us and brought us food at least once each day. Meanwhile—as we heard only much later—my husband, András got back to Budapest from the labor camp. Somewhere, in one of the streets of the city, he was caught. That is how he was taken to Buchenwald, where he perished. We learned all this only long after the war, as we also did about the fate of my parents and my younger brother Bandi. Father, Mother, and Bandi were deported together from the Nyiregyháza ghetto; my parents perished in Auschwitz and Bandi in Dachau. My first son, who was born from my second marriage, is named Andy, after my brother.

ZOLTAN

The Jewish High Holiday season of 1944 began in the middle of September, a month before that bloody October day when the "Arrow Cross" gang virtually took over Hungary. We were still together then, at Aunt Aranka's apartment; and we held our Rosh Hashanah and Yom Kippur services right there, at Akacfa 6. The men in our family, including my grandfather, Henrick Zucker, plus several other men from the building, made up our *minyan*—the ten adult men without which a traditional Jewish prayer service cannot be held. We used a Torah scroll we'd found in the street; it must have come from one of the synagogues that had been closed and abandoned. We even had two cantors: very nice young men from Poland who were living "underground," with forged Aryan papers, in a non-Jewish neighborhood.

At about that time rumors started that Hungary was ready to make a separate peace with Russia. That was when the "Arrow Cross" movement suddenly took over. The Jews in Budapest were placed under a curfew—they could only leave their homes for shopping and other errands between 10:00 A.M. and 4:00 or 5:00 P.M. But now the Jews weren't safe even during those hours. The "Arrow Cross" gangs were not only picking up Jews in the streets but also broke into the "Jewish houses" and dragged the tenants from their beds.

By that time our textile mill was out of business for good,

because there weren't any people left to work there. I got in touch with Gyula Adonyi, a very nice gentile man who lived next door to my factory with his wife. He was a cabinetmaker, and his workshop was connected by a door and window with one of the stockrooms of my factory. I asked Mr. Adonyi whether he would be willing to help my family if things became really bad for the Jews. "After all," I said to him, "it can't last much longer. The Russians are coming closer all the time and sooner or later the Germans will be out." Of course, I said, I realized that helping my family might put Adonyi and his wife into danger, but Mr. Adonyi said, "I like you; you've always been very good to me, letting me use your telephone and doing me other favors. I'll do whatever I can for you and your family."

Meanwhile, whatever was still left of Hungarian independence came to an end. The "Arrow Cross" people took charge officially under Ferenc Szálasi, who became the dictator of Hungary. Admiral Horthy—the admiral without a fleet and regent without a kingdom—was arrested along with his cabinet. The Nazis deported him to Germany. That was where American troops eventually caught up with him. He was put into jail in Nuremberg, but he was never tried with the rest of the war criminals. He was released but couldn't go back to Hungary because by that time the Communists were in charge there. So he went into exile in Portugal, where he died in 1957.

After the High Holidays, I had to go through another spell of labor camp duty. I played sick again. A couple of hundred men —some really sick, some just "sick" like me, with faked medical certificates you could still get for money—were organized into a "sick brigade" and marched to Transdanubia, in the western part of Hungary. We marched about 50 miles; the march took us four days because most of the people in the brigade were genuinely handicapped—either by sickness or by old age. We stopped at a place near Lake Balaton, where the fashionable Budapest Jews spent their summer vacations before the war. There, the Germans quartered us in several abandoned farmhouses and put us to work digging ditches. They said these were to be trenches for the German soldiers, who'd soon have to dig in at this spot because the Russians were coming. We were also told that the bombs were falling on Budapest all the time.

The Germans didn't treat us too badly. Some of our guards* were not even Germans, but Austrians, who hated Hitler and the whole war. Like most Hungarian Jews of my generation, I spoke a good German and so I started a conversation with one of the Austrian guards. The man cursed the war. All he wanted was to be back home in Austria, with his wife and children. He really couldn't care less about the Jews, one way or the other.

One day—it was November 9 or 10—I heard rumors that we'd be moved out of our village soon. The story was that we'd be marched out of Hungary and into Germany proper. One of my campmates was our friend, Willy Grosz, who'd moved into Aunt Aranka's apartment with his wife, Ethel. He'd been caught and put into the labor camp when all Jews from the age of 16 to 60 had to report for labor service. Willy and I were sure that if we didn't use this opportunity to escape, it would be the end for us.

I remember the day we escaped. It was a rainy Friday morning. It rained so hard that our ditch-digging details couldn't go out to work. Three or four of us, including Willy Grosz and myself, hit upon an idea. We went to the Austrian guard with whom I'd made friends and I said to him, "There are four of us here with dental problems. Our teeth hurt like hell. We'd like to go the nearest town and see a dentist." The guard offered to let us go to the next town with a horse and buggy driven by one of the German soldiers. We'd have to pay him something, of course, he said. In return, the German soldier would take us into town, wait while we found a dentist, and then bring us back to our temporary camp in the village. We made the trip into town, but what we looked for was a railroad station, not a dentist. When we arrived at the station, we found out that no trains were running anymore. We were ready to give up and return to the village. Then we saw some people standing at the shoulder of the road. I wanted to know what they were waiting for, but naturally I didn't dare approach strangers while I had the yellow Star of

---

*This was the so-called Todt organization, mostly older and reservists soldier, a bit more human than the Wehrmacht.

David pinned to my coat. I said to our German soldier who was waiting for us nearby, "You wait a moment; I want to go over there and get some information." The German didn't seem to care. "Go," he said. So I unpinned my star to go over to these people. Just then an SS truck pulled up, stopped, and the people began to pile into it. I jumped on the SS truck. My three friends, including Willy Grosz, took my cue. They ripped off their Stars of David also and leaped onto the SS truck after me. Luckily, neither the driver of the truck, nor any of the other passengers already on the truck, paid attention to us. The truck driver didn't ask anyone for identification papers. If he had asked us, it would have been our end, because none of us four fugitives had any papers. But by that time things were chaotic in the Hungarian countryside, and it appeared that even German efficiency wasn't working anymore.

We didn't know where the SS truck was headed and we didn't care, as long as we could escape from our "sick brigade." After a while it got dark, but I could make out where we were going. We were traveling in the direction of Budapest! This was certainly our lucky day! Soon, we were inside the city and the truck stopped near a curb. Everyone got off, and so did we. Willy and I jumped aboard a passing streetcar and went straight to Aunt Aranka's apartment on Akacfa 6. By that time the Sabbath had begun, and when we arrived at the apartment, Uncle Endre was just reciting the *kiddush* before the Friday night dinner. You can imagine the surprise; Willy's wife and my sister Eva, and everybody else, too, was overjoyed.

But the rejoicing did not last long. That was the weekend when the Germans began to evacuate the "Jewish houses," and those Jews who were still free had to move into even more cramped quarters. Now we had to quit Akacfa 6. Uncle Endre and Aunt Aranka had Swedish papers, so they moved into one of the "Swedish houses." I had Swiss papers, but they were worthless. If you were challenged, the Swiss representatives never defended the documents. I wanted to be with my sister, who "only" had faked Aryan papers. I got in touch with my friends the Adonyis, who were still living next door to my textile mill. I went out to see them; I made the trip from Budapest by commuters' train, just as I used to when I still went to the factory. Before I reached the station, I took off my Star of David. Luck was with me once more; nobody stopped me or asked me for identification.

I asked Mr. Adonyi whether he would be able to hide four people: Eva, two of her girlfriends, and me. Mr. Adonyi said it would not be easy; especially, there would be problems with food. But he would manage somehow. All he asked was that we wait until after dark to move into our hideout. I took the next train back to Budapest and helped Eva and the two other girls pack. Not that we had much baggage; each of us carried only one rucksack that was filled with our most necessary personal belongings. We waited until the evening to go to the station, and even then we made sure to use only back streets and alleys, where no one would notice us.

Mr. Adonyi was waiting for us. He'd already put a lock on the door between his workshop and the stockroom of my factory. The stockroom was to be our home, under the Adonyis' protection. Mr. Adonyi had put in some mattresses, but that was all. We didn't even have running water. Mr. Adonyi locked the door from the outside, and we pasted heavy paper over the window between our stockroom and the Adonyis' workshop so that if we'd have to put on a light after dark, people outside shouldn't notice.

The Adonyis were wonderful people. Twice each day—in the morning and again at night—they would open the window between their workshop and our hideout and pass us food. Supper was always a hot meal. I talked to Mr. Adonyi through the window and handed him whatever cash I still possessed to buy food and other supplies for us. The whole thing was very risky for Mr. Adonyi. He didn't have ration cards for four extra people, of course; so he had to buy our food on the black market. In addition to the danger this involved, it cost a lot of money. After a while I ran out of cash. I knew that Mr. Adonyi was a poor man and wouldn't be able to lend us money, but I remembered another gentile man I used to know, who was a little better off. I gave Mr. Adonyi the address of his man. Much to my relief, he was willing to advance some money to Mr. Adonyi and he agreed to wait until we could reimburse him—"when things get a little more settled," he said, meaning, of course, after the Germans had gone from Budapest.

As the end of 1944 approached, the situation deteriorated rapidly. Budapest was in a state of siege. All Allies were bombing the city around the clock. The Russians had come close enough to shell the suburbs from the ground with their long-range artillery. Russian shells kept exploding all around Adonyis' place and our hideout and I was beginning to think that the four of us would never live to see the liberation. If we were to survive, we'd have to find a new hiding place, not in the suburbs but inside the city, where we'd only have the air raids to worry about, because the Russians were not yet within artillery range of downtown Budapest.

I found out that friends of my family—their name was Freund —were hiding in the city, in a building on Hungaria Körut, an elegant boulevard in a fine gentile neighborhood. (Budapest's best residential neighborhoods were in the downtown section.) I made contact with the Freunds, and they let us know that they would have room at least for Eva.

The day came when we had no other choice but to take advantage of the Freunds' offer. German and Hungarian soldiers set up camp in the courtyard of my factory. One evening they broke into Mr. Adonyi's basement and looked around for food. Mr. Adonyi was afraid they'd discover our stockroom—and us. So he kept following them wherever they went, insisting, "There's no food here, and also no people." After that, Mr. Adonyi agreed that at least Eva and her two girlfriends should move to the city. And he was nice enough to escort the three girls by train to the city, to the Freunds' house on Hungaria Körut. I bade farewell to them and stayed on, alone, in this stockroom of my factory, next to the Adonyis.

KLÁRI

My mother, my little daughter Zsuzsi, and I stayed at Aranka Lowy's apartment until October 1944. Then we hid out for a while in the workshop of my brother Pista's factory in the City Hall building. From there we went to the home of my gentile sister-in-law Gizi, on the other side of town, on Jozsika Street. We spent three bitter months with Gizi. I say "bitter" because we lived in terribly cramped quarters, with no heat, hardly any food, and in constant fear. This, of course, wasn't Gizi's fault; the circumstances were to blame. Actually, we spent most of our time not in Gizi's apartment but in the air raid shelter of her building. We didn't really mind the bombs; we wished that there should be more and more air raids all the time, because that would mean we'd be liberated that much sooner.

Meanwhile, my husband Tibor, for whom I'd obtained Swedish papers, found shelter in one of the "Swedish houses."

TIBOR

How did I first learn about that Swedish nobleman, Raoul Wallenberg, who saved so many Hungarian Jews from the Germans? It was when my wife Klári came to me in the hospital in Budapest and told me the good news that we'd become Swedish citizens, and I was a free man, because Sweden was neutral, and the Germans respected that. I moved straight from the army hospital into one of the "Swedish houses" which Wallenberg, who was attached to the Swedish embassy in Budapest, set aside as havens for Jews. I still remember the address of my particular "Swedish house." It was on Ulloi utca 4. The building had a big Swedish emblem on the front door. Inside, there were about 300 escapees. They all slept on the floor; the daily food ration was about one bowlful of bean soup per person. I can assure you that no one in that building had to worry about a reducing diet!

After I'd been at Ulloi utca a few days, Wallenberg himself appeared. He was very thin, distinguished-looking, youngish but beginning to grow bald. He kept his distance from people, but he was friendly and acted really concerned about the Jews whose lives he was trying to save. Wallenberg had come to Ulloi utca to select what he called a "protocol group" from among the Jews that were hiding out in the building.

I was among those picked for the "protocol group." Why? First of all, I was comparatively young, only 31 years old. Also, and maybe even more important, I did not look Jewish. Our group was supposed to work very closely with Wallenberg on special missions. Some of our men were given monks' habits or priests' cassocks to put on. In this disguise we would enter the buildings where the "Arrow Cross" troops were keeping Jews they'd picked up in the streets.

At other times Wallenberg sent our group to one of Budapest's major railroad terminals. At a certain station, the Jozsefváros, we had to surround the railroad tracks in a circle of about 200 meters and wait until transports of Jews came into the station, for deportation to a labor camp—or worse. As soon as these unlucky Jews arrived at the train platform, we had to move closer and shout that whoever had Swedish or Swiss papers should follow us. At first, these poor people didn't understand, but eventually they got the idea. Even though most of them had no documents whatsoever, they'd follow us and we'd pretend to be checking their papers. For appearances' sake we'd tell them to hand us any slips of paper they happened to have in their pockets—medical prescriptions, personal letters, anything. And then we'd "pass" them and take them away with us, to one of the "Swedish" or "Swiss" houses in the city.

On one of these missions I had an opportunity to observe at first hand what a calm, brave man Wallenberg was. Early one morning, at dawn, two other men and I received orders from Wallenberg to go to Jokai utca 4, formerly the headquarters of the Travelers' Associates. That building had been taken over by the "Arrow Cross" party and inside there were three battalions of Jews ready to leave for the railroad station to be deported. We entered the building, checked in with the German officers and told them that we were from the Swedish consulate. As representatives of a neutral country, of course, we were admitted at once. Our orders were to wait until Wallenberg would join us, and then we would try to save as many of the Jews as we could from deportation. But by eight o'clock Wallenberg had not yet arrived, and the German officers had begun to line up the Jews for departure. Then, at 8:15, we saw Wallenberg's big, black diplomatic limousine approaching. The three of us ran toward the car and told Wallenberg that there was no time to lose. Wallenberg calmed us down; he said he could handle the situation. He told us to let the Germans go ahead with the march to the station. He also ordered us to join the other Jews and walk with them. When the transport started out, eight rucksacks remained on the sidewalk in front of the Travelers' Associates Building. This meant that eight men had managed to escape.

Wallenberg waited for the line of deportees to move off. Then he started his car, driving very, very slowly, stopping every 500 meters or so to let the marching line catch up with him.

When we arrived at the railroad station, the three of us placed ourselves close to the train platform and got ready to do our usual routine—shout that whoever had Swiss or Swedish papers should leave the line and step over to us to have their papers checked. As usual, Wallenberg left, because he did not want to be too visible at the station.

Then—disaster. Three big German military cars pulled up near the train platform. The doors opened, and several SS officers jumped out, dressed in the special SS uniforms and raincoats. They shouted at us that we were out of bounds. No unauthorized persons were permitted near the train platform while Jews were put aboard a deportation train.

The three of us stood there, white, shaking like leaves, not knowing what would happen next. A few moments later, Wallenberg himself appeared, also white as a sheet, but in perfect command of himself. He started a big argument with the SS officers, explaining that he'd had an agreement with the German authorities that he and his men could be on the train platform at any time to protect citizens of Sweden. After all, the Germans respected the neutrality of Sweden, a country that was doing them plenty of favors. In the end, the three of us and others were allowed to go.

This incident did not cramp Wallenberg's style. The activities of our "protocol group" continued as before, and many more hundreds of Jews were saved.

MARIANNE

On the day before New Year's Eve, 1944–45, I must have been the last to clean out whatever was still left in the delicatessen store I passed on my daily visits to Pista in the Swedish consulate. I bought bread, hot dogs, salami and whatever else was available— holiday delicacies for Pista and the others. That day things really were bad in the streets; with the shells and the bombs and ma- chine-gunning from low flying planes, I didn't know how I'd get to the consulate alive. It was insane for civilians to be out in the streets of downtown Budapest. People were no longer living in their apartments; they spent 24 hours of each day in the air raid shelters. So on New Year's Eve I decided I wasn't going to return to the Tabaks' apartment at all but would move in with Pista at the Swedish consulate.

I took with me only my most important personal belongings. The clothes I put on for the move were all the clothes I now possessed—a rather colorful outfit, I must say; a plaid skirt with a vest and blouse and, because it was quite cold, I wore under the skirt one of Pista's slacks. Under the slacks I wore my last pair of nylon stockings, along with a pair of boots. This whole outfit was covered by the one beautiful thing I still owned, an elegant winter coat, a kind of beige olive color with a big collar and cuffs of nutria. The coat was stylish and chic when I bought it; it had been part of my trousseau. I don't remember what I wore on my head; I think it was a kerchief. Women didn't bother with hats anymore.

At the consulate I unpacked the food I had brought with me and we had a kind of New Year's Eve party. I was only sorry that my parents and grandfather couldn't be there. My parents' "Swedish house" was in a different part of the city. My grandfather's apartment building hadn't been designated as a "Jewish house," so he and his wife, Hilda, were among the first to be moved into the ghetto after the "Arrow Cross" took over on October 15. At first we were able to communicate with my parents from time to time and even to send them a little money. But we knew nothing about Grandfather and Hilda. We could only hope that they were alive and unhurt. Nevertheless, we tried to keep up our spirits that New Year's Eve. We knew that our liberators must be very near, because of the constant bombings. We were sure it couldn't last much longer; it was just a matter of time—*Schicksal*—fate.

Raoul Wallenberg personally took charge of the people who hid out in the Swedish consulate building. Most of us who were hidden there quickly got accustomed to our quarters. We lived in the basement air-raid shelters. Our day-to-day lives consisted of trying to stretch the supply of staple foods that was available —mostly powdered eggs, canned tomatoes, and such. There were many of us, but the shelter was big, so we weren't really cramped together, but sanitary facilities were as good as non-existent. We got our water from the one sink that was available. Every individual was assigned a daily ration of about a quarter of a bucket of water for washing and drinking. I still remember how I divided up my own water ration. I used some of it for brushing my teeth, and some for washing my face and the upper part of my body. Then I put all that water into a basin and gave myself a mini-bath, and after that I used it again as wash water for my underwear and my "lace" stockings—I mean my one pair of nylons which by then were so full of runs that they looked like lace! Because they were my last pair of stockings, I didn't have the heart to throw them away. I felt that as long as I wore a pair of clean hose, no matter how torn, and clean underwear, I was decent and could look the world in the face. The saddest casualty of those days in the Swedish consulate shelter was my beautiful winter coat, which I had to wear almost all the time because of the cold and the constant draft in the basement. When we stood in line for the red liquid that was supposed to pass for tomato soup, and the yellow scrambled-egg mixture made from the powdered eggs, I couldn't help getting food stains on my coat, so my elegant coat soon had a colorful print pattern that had never been intended and that couldn't be removed with the little water I had at my disposal.

People didn't socialize too much in the shelter. The only man who became a good friend to Pista and me was the violinist Victor Aitay, who was hidden with us in the consulate and worked as telephone operator for the building.

VICTOR AITAY

Victor Aitay acted as the telephone operator in the Swedish consulate building where Marianne, Pista, and hundreds others were hidden during the siege of Budapest. Born of a mixed marriage—a Jewish father and a gentile mother—Aitay is an internationally-known violinist today, the co-concertmaster of the Chicago Symphony Orchestra. Had it not been for Raoul Wallenberg, Aitay might not have survived the war and the musical world would have been deprived of an outstanding talent.

*Victor was what you'd call a "child prodigy." He began to study the violin when he was five and graduated from the Franz Liszt Academy of Budapest with an artist's diploma. During the war his parents were safe because his mother was a gentile, so she could hide his father. He himself wasn't so fortunate; he spent three years, on and off, in labor camps. Those were three agonizing years—aside from the hardships and the fear for the lives of his loved ones, there was the punishment of not being able to touch his violin. Three years is a long time for a punishment like that.

At first he was in Erdély, Transylvania, which is part of Hungary. There his group of inmates spent a year at heavy manual labor, digging rocks from the ground and moving them from one place to another. This was ridiculous; it didn't make any sense.

*Anonymous testimony

Later, when the Hungarian army was called to the battlefront, they were moved into the hills and were put to work pushing tanks with their own hands over terrain that the cumbersome tanks couldn't negotiate without help. They had to keep up with the army and the motorized vehicles, and had to do it on foot. This caused many casualties because those who were elderly or not so strong and who collapsed on the highway were shot then and there. The same thing happened to anyone who dared break ranks and stop at a village well for a drink of water. Whoever survived must have been a special favorite of God's.

Many tried to escape. One of his friends managed to do it, disguised as a priest. Victor also tried to escape, but he was recaptured twice; finally, in his third escape, he made it to Budapest. He went to the Swedish consulate where Raoul Wallenberg —whom he considers one of the greatest heroes of our times— gave him a Swedish passport and the job of telephone operator. He was put in charge of the inside switchboard and handled whatever outside calls there were.

MARIANNE

One day in January 1945, luck ran out for my husband, Pista. I remember that two or three of us left the basement of the Swedish consulate to go up to the third or fourth floor—I don't remember which—of the building. The building had been pretty badly bombed, and only some parts remained intact. A doctor was working in one of these rooms, attending to anyone who needed medical services. He had, I think, some anti-flu vaccine. Pista was downstairs in the shelter; I told him to come up with me, but he wouldn't come. He was busy at the sink, peering into a piece of mirror glass and trying to give himself a shave. The idea of a flu shot at this stage did not appeal to him, but I thought: Why not?

Suddenly, I heard a big commotion out in the street. We rushed to the window, looked out and saw "Arrow Cross" men heading straight for the air-raid shelter. Five minutes later we saw a long line of people being marched out from the basement, including Pista. I was certain that I'd seen the last of my husband; by that time the Nazis didn't even bother to take Jews to prison or to deport them. There was no other way; the Russians were coming closer all the time. So whenever the "Arrow Cross" or the Germans got hold of Jews, they simply marched them off to the banks of the Danube and shot them into the river.

But Victor Aitay, the telephone operator, knew what to do. He had a secret number to call in the event of an emergency. Through this number, he let Wallenberg's staff know what had happened to the people in the basement. As we heard later, Wallenberg himself jumped into his limousine and drove at top speed to the banks of the Danube. He walked right up to the German officers and made it clear to them that the prisoners were under the protection of the kingdom of Sweden, of which he was the official representative. His manner and his way of talking to them put fear into the hearts of them and they must have decided it was best not to antagonize the Swedes. They must have realized that the war would soon be over for them, and perhaps the Swedes would be good for some favors when the Russians came. At any rate, they told all the Jewish prisoners to line up and escorted them back to the Swedish consulate. And so my husband, too, came back. One of the men—his name was Schossberger—later told us that he'd had with him a huge diamond which his mother had given him. Well, when he was marched away from the consulate to the Danube, he was so sure the end was coming for him that he didn't want the diamond to fall into German hands. So, as they were marched away, he threw it into the snow, which was falling thick and fast. Now he was sorry he'd given up so quickly. Maybe this is a lesson; as long as there is life, there is hope. Don't throw your hands up in despair and don't throw away your last possessions.

TIBOR

I will never forgot that day in January 1945, when the end almost
came for my brother-in-law Pista Reiss, I and all the others who
had been hiding out in the Swedish consulate. I also was able to
observe at first hand how Raoul Wallenberg saved them. A troop
of "Arrow Cross" men entered the Swedish consulate and
rounded up the Jews inside. They told the Jews not to bother
about taking any personal belongings with them, because where
they were going they wouldn't need anything anymore. This was
very early on a cold, snowy morning, around dawn. The "Arrow
Cross" people lined up all the men and women, on the street. The
Hungarians claimed that the air raid shelter was not part of the
embassy, and that therefore they could do with the Jews in the
shelter as they pleased. Wallenberg wasn't there at the time. I and
some others from the "protocol group" made a fast getaway and
hid behind the bombed-out ruins. Unfortunately we could do
nothing but watch and wait in fear and trembling and make sure
that no one saw us.

At around three o'clock that afternoon, all of a sudden, we saw
the long line of hundreds of Jews marching up the street, back
to the consulate. They were all there, completely unharmed,
including Pista. We learned afterwards that Wallenberg himself
had gone to the banks of the Danube and ordered the "Arrow
Cross" officers to let these people go because they were under the
protection of the Swedish government.

During those final days of the siege of Budapest, in January 1945, I myself had a narrow escape. The bombing and shelling were so constant that we stayed in the basement of Ulloi utca and hardly ever went upstairs. But one day the leaders of our "protocol group" called a conference on the second floor. Just as we were ready to climb up to the second floor, there was a loud blast. The door through which we were going to enter the "conference room" broke off and half the building fell down, so there was no place for us to go anymore. If we had passed there a split second later, we all would have been killed.

Marianne (engagement picture, 1943)

Aranka and Endre Lowy, 1946

Sitting L-R: Endre, Aranka, Henrick, Hilda, Zsuzsi, Gizella Reiss

Standing L-R: Zoltan, Steven, Marianne, Jack Friedman, Eva, Charles (Chanukah, Budapest 1946)

Zucker Family "Tree of life," by Barbara Treitel

Marianne, age 16, first ball. Ball gown by Wallenstein, photograph by
Hedy Rezsnyi

A PESTI IZR. HITKÖZSÉG LEÁNYGIMNÁZIUMA
VIII. OSZTÁLYÁNAK NÖVENDÉKEI.

1942   1943

The last class (1943) to graduate from the Girls Jewish Gymnasium, Budapest, as then established.

Family: Cilla, Ferenc and Lucy Ullman; Bandi, Rozsi, Eva, Mor and Zoltan Weisz; Aranka, Andrew and Marianne Lowy

Pauline Metzger

Stephen (Pista) Reiss

Pauline and Nathan Zucker

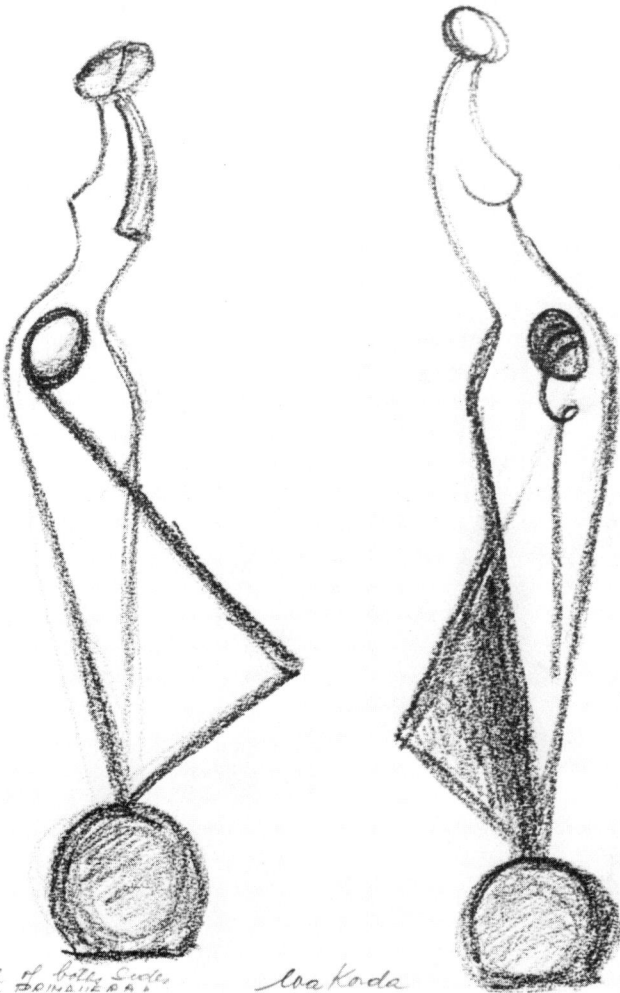

Sketch of both scales
PRIMAVERA

Eva Korda

Primavera, Eva Weisz Korda

Primavera photo-Eva Weisz Korda

the Vayda family in U.S.

ZOLTAN

By Christmas 1944, you could almost go crazy from the bombing. I was still in my old hideout, the stockroom of my factory, next to the Adonyis' workshop. One day part of my factory got hit; it was almost a direct hit, but the stockroom was still there, and so was I.

On January 3, 1945, I was reciting my daily morning prayers as usual. I still had my *tallith* and *tefillin** and put them on each morning, without fail, no matter what was happening outside. Well, on that morning, while I was praying, there was a loud knock on the door of the stockroom. It was Mr. Adonyi. I interrupted my prayers. "What happened?" I asked. "Come out, Mr. Weiss! It's all right to come out!" Mr. Adonyi yelled. "The Russians are here!" So I opened the door slowly, and I went out. And really, there were the Russians. Russian soldiers all over the place.

But our happiness lasted for only about one day, because suddenly the Germans counterattacked. You have never seen such a sight—the Russians were retreating with their horses, their armored vehicles, their bicycles, and even on foot. They were running away from our suburb like crazy, retreating because the Germans were shelling them with their long-range artillery from inside the city.

*Prayer shawl and phylacteries.

Mr. Adonyi was really scared because by now all the people in the neighborhood knew that he'd been giving shelter to Jews. He said, "I really don't know what to do now. Maybe I should leave this place and follow the Russians. Or should I stay here? I really don't know. But you, Mr. Weiss, you must get out of here! So try to meet up with the Russians and follow them wherever they go. That way you'll at least have a chance of escaping the Germans."

Across the street from my hideout there was a big oil refinery. I figured that the Russians wouldn't give up that place without a fight. So I didn't leave. And really, that's where the Russians decided to hold the line. The officers drew their pistols and didn't allow any of their men to run away. So I thought I was safe at last, and no one noticed me.

But once the Russians held the line, other troubles came. The Russians started picking up people in the street and placing them under arrest.

Now the Adonyis had an only son, who had been married only a short time and lived six or seven blocks away from his parents, nearer to the city. One day Mr. Adonyi came to me and said he hadn't heard from his son and daughter-in-law for days and he'd like to go to their house and see whether they were all right. But he wanted me to go with him; he figured the Russians might not pick him up if he wasn't alone.

I didn't think it was the right time yet. We were close to the highway and could see the confusion; people were arrested and shot, right and left.

But about four days later I said to Mr. Adonyi, "We might as well try it now." And so Mr. Adonyi and I went on the highway, toward his son's house.

A Russian military policeman stopped us, a young fellow. "*Papiere! Papiere!* (Papers! Papers!)" he said to us. Probably he thought we wouldn't know Russian but maybe we'd understand German. I answered him, "*Keine Papiere! Keine Papiere!* (I have no documents on me.)" Then I took a wild chance. I started talking to this Russian not in German but in Yiddish. My guess turned out to be correct, because he replied in Yiddish.

"*Vus zugst di?* (What are you saying?)" he asked. Then, "*Ver bizt di?* (Who are you?)"

So I told him, "*Ikh bin a yid!* (I'm a Jew)."

"*Di bist a yid?* (So you're Jewish?)" the Russian replied. "*Vi kimst di her?* (How did you get here, to this place?)"

When I explained to him that I'd been in hiding, he asked, "*Vi voinst di?* (Where do you live?)"

I told him the whole story. Then he said, still in Yiddish, "We're picking up everybody we find in the street. Who's this man with you?" He pointed to Mr. Adonyi.

"Don't worry about him," I said. "He's all right."

The Russian told me to go back to the place where I lived. It was dangerous to be out if you had no papers, he said. He'd come to visit me. And he told me one more thing: "Don't open the door for anybody. My name is Miller. My Jewish name is Zvi. When I come, I'll knock on the door and yell 'Zvi!' Then you can open." So Mr. Adonyi and I didn't go to his son's place that day.

That same evening Zvi came to visit Mr. Adonyi and me, and gave us a pair of safe-conduct passes, so we could go out in the street without fear of being picked up by Russian soldiers. And so, the next day, Mr. Adonyi and I went out to visit his son. The young couple was fine. They'd been hiding in the apartment; they were starved, but they'd survived.

The day after that, Mr. Adonyi was nice enough to go into the city, pick up my sister Eva from the Freunds' hideout on Hungaria Körut, and escort her back to our place. In the evening Zvi came again, wearing a huge army coat. Under that coat he had bags full of bread, salami and eggs—whatever you could want after months of starving! When Zvi saw Eva, he asked, "Who's that girl?"

When I told him she was my sister, he said, "*Ikh gloib nisht* (I don't believe you). There are no Jewish girls left." Then he burst out crying. "I had two sisters in Leningrad, and they both were killed." Eva had to recite all the Hebrew prayers she knew, and the Hebrew alphabet, to prove that she was really Jewish. Zvi was still crying, and now he told us that his father lived in Cracow, in Poland, where he'd been a *shochet,* a ritual slaughterer.

From that time on Zvi brought us whatever good things he could "organize"—that was the word we used for "steal," in those those days. He knocked on our door sometimes as often as three times a day, and he had shoes, clothing, and food under his coat. He'd walk in, drop his gifts on the floor, and then leave again, fast.

Around January 15, I figured that by now it might be safe to go to the city. Of course, I couldn't know for sure, because there was no radio, no way of communicating. But I decided to try it; I wanted to find my grandfather, Aunt Aranka, and the rest of the family.

I got to the city without being stopped.

The first familiar face I saw in the city was that of Tibor Grosz, the son of our friend Willy Grosz. The Germans had retreated from Pest to the Buda side of the Danube and were shelling Pest from there. Still, Tibor and I kept close to the river, because we wanted to go to the apartment where my grandfather and Hilda had lived before the Germans moved them into the ghetto.

But we were stopped by a couple of Russian soldiers carrying a case of ammunition. They put their load down on the ground, pointed to it and ordered, "Carry!" This was no good, carrying explosives when the shells were whizzing all around us. I happened to know that particular neighborhood well. I looked behind me and saw that the Russian soldiers hadn't been able to keep up with us. So I said to Tibor, "Follow me!" and we ducked into one of the side streets. Somewhere along the way, we gently put down the case of explosives and ran away, very fast.

MARIANNE

The first liberation of Budapest came one day late in January 1945. I don't remember the exact date anymore. I only remember how the Russian troops entered the Swedish consulate. We were all in the air raid shelter, and that's where the Russians came in—through the basement. The ones who came in first were something like an advance guard. I remember that they were officers, not run-of-the-mill soldiers.

The fighting spread from street to street, from house to house, from basement to basement. The Swedish consulate was a very large building. It was quadrangular, built around a courtyard like all the old-style European houses.

We were in the cellar and that is where the Russian officers made their first appearance. They said they were advance guards of the Red Army, that we were now liberated and that we had nothing to worry about anymore. At least that's how the interpreter who was with the officers translated it. I understood only one word that the one officer repeated over and over again, "*Kultura, kultura.*" In other words, these Russian officers wanted to tell us that they were high officials, really cultured people, not nobodies. But after one "*kultura,*" spat on the floor which showed that he, at least, wasn't so cultured after all.

We had made ourselves some primitive candles, from ropes around which we put some hard fat. After the officer had finished his long speech, he took my candle and left the cellar with it, leaving us in total darkness. The next morning, when some light was beginning to shine through the little basement window, I discovered that my overnight bag, which contained my last items of civilization such as a change of panties, and my comb and brush, and toothbrush, and which I'd always kept close by me, was missing. Probably the "cultured" Russian had needed a gift for one of his girlfriends!

The next morning, something much worse happened. The Germans came back! Swedish flag or no Swedish flag, they occupied our building. The Swedish consulate and its courtyard became a battlefield where the Russians and the Germans were shooting it out. We were in the middle, lined up, caught in the crossfire. The bullets were flying past our ears, and if it wasn't bullets, it was artillery shells. It must have been like that in the trenches, on the battlefields. Only God knows how we survived.

But then, all of a sudden, there was quiet. The Russians took over and the Germans gave up. The German soldiers were taking off their uniforms and were holding up civilians in the street for civilian clothing; they wanted to mingle among the population, to escape punishment from the Russians.

That was our second liberation. But it was not yet the end of our troubles. We could hardly heave a deep sigh of relief when, instead of the high-ranking officers, Russian foot soldiers started to trample into our basement and everybody was lined up and there was a fellow who was from the Ukraine among us . . . I don't know whether he was there before, or maybe he came from another building. Because by then, you know, everybody was running from one basement to another, so, really, we weren't sure anymore just who was who.

Anyway, whoever survived started to come in from other basements. Like mice, you know, crawling out of their holes and looking around. So, this man who, I think, was from the Ukraine talked Russian and taught me Russian words. He said, "You just keep saying these words when the Russian soldiers come." I said, "Why?" So, he gave me a fast course on the Russians. The soldiers, he said, would rape every woman, but if I said I was a Jewish woman, then, I might be saved. So I learned the words *Ievrei,* or something like that.

We lined up. You must visualize the basement, full of cubicles. We were pushed from one cubicle into another and the Russians counted the people, for God knows what reason. And then we went into yet another cubicle in the basement. I noticed that the Russians were just sorting out women and taking them into another cubicle. And then—I don't know whether it was the same Ukrainian fellow or another Russian—taught me another Russian word. I think he had realized by then that being Jewish wouldn't help me because we were mostly all Jewish. The Russian word he taught me was *klapetz*, which means "child." This, I guess, means in Russian "With child," or "pregnant." So I said *"klapetz"* and walked into the other room, but soon I realized that this might not be enough to save me. It was absolutely devastating; that after one horror such other horrors should come. There seemed to be no end to it.

I hid under one of the cots—maybe it was even my own—and stayed there, without moving from the spot, for three days.

The women lived in sheer terror of the Russians; women of all ages took to wearing babushkas and put this horrible paint on their faces, whatever they could find—coals, I don't know, just to make themselves as ugly and as old as possible, but nothing helped. But I was very fortunate. The Russian-speaking man, the one who taught me to say *"klapetz,"* really did save me.

After three days, the Russians soldiers left our basement. Other troops came in their place, but we were able to emerge from the shelter. Pista and I wanted to go to Akacfa 6 to see whether the house was still standing and whether my parents were all right. The streets were an incredible sight. There were dead horses, probably from the cavalry, literally piled up on street corners. And people were tip-toeing out from corners and basements, sneaking up to the dead horses, cutting off hunks of horsemeat to feed themselves. Here and there a stray bullet whistled past us, but as we went farther into the city, it became quieter and quieter because that part had already been liberated earlier.

Pista and I never touched a dead horse. I don't really recall what we ate during those first days of liberation. I didn't consider food all that important. Maybe I had crackers or pieces of chocolate, from the supplies we'd stored up for the siege. The food was half-spoiled, but still safe to eat. So Pista and I survived. There are times in life when it really doesn't matter to you—you don't realize it—whether or not you eat. You forget all about food. All you care about is reaching your goal, your destination. In my case, that destination was Akacfa 6, my parents' house.

TIBOR

I was one of the unlucky people who got wounded after the
Germans left Budapest.

The night after the first Russians came into the house on Ulloi
utca 4, we went to sleep on the floor of the basement air raid
shelter, happy in the belief that we were free at last. For the first
time in weeks, some of us figured it was safe to take off our outer
clothes.

But then, after midnight, we heard loud voices speaking in
Hungarian. An entire "Arrow Cross" gang had taken over our
part of the "Swedish house." They shot bullets into the walls of
the building, probably to scare us. At dawn they ordered us all
to come out of the basement, and then they put us through a
"selection," as the Germans used to do in the concentration
camps. The Jews were commanded to step to one side. The few
gentiles that were in the building were commanded to stand on
the other side. Since I look anything but Jewish, I pretended to
be a gentile. After this "selection," the "Arrow Cross" men told
everybody, Jews and gentiles, to get going and they said, "Now
we're going to shoot you all, one by one." They were in high
spirits; they brought lots of liquor with them, which you could
smell from ten feet away. Before the war, there'd been a girls'
boarding school on the fifth floor of the house. A few of the
Jewish girls from that school were in the building, hiding out.
They marched out of the shelter along with the others, but the

"Arrow Cross" men began to flirt and drink with the girls, until both the men and the girls were roaring drunk.

Meanwhile, some of us reached the other side of the "Swedish house" and saw—to our amazement—a bowl full of apples. We fell on the fruit. After a while, those "Arrow Cross" men who were still able to see and walk straight turned their attention from the girls back to us. They began to march people out from this part of the basement, too. They took one young man out of the building, and shortly thereafter we heard shots, but later we found out that they didn't kill the man.

At nightfall, our final liberation came. The Russians reoccupied the building. It was a miracle that none of us were harmed before, but this was the time fate caught up with me.

I looked out into the street. I didn't see any Germans, or any "Arrow Cross" men, around. I wanted to go to my sister-in-law's apartment on Jozsika Street, where my wife, Klári, our little daughter and my mother-in-law were hiding. Two other men and I left the "Swedish" house and picked our way carefully, from one bombed-out shell to the next. We turned off into a broad boulevard and approached Jozsika Street. On the way, we met some Russians who grabbed our wrist watches. If we hadn't given them the watches, they'd probably have shot us then and there.

Suddenly there was a loud explosion. That's when I got three pieces of shrapnel in my knee. I bled very badly, but I kept going, crawling on my good leg. I made it to Jozsika Street, and there were Klári, little Zsuzsi, and her mother, alive and well.

ARANKA

My husband and I spent the last months of the German occupation in one of the "Swedish houses," on Katona Jozsef utca. My daughter and my son-in-law were at the Swedish consulate. Sometimes I did not hear from them for days and days. It was good they were in the Swedish consulate building; this way, at least, they were able to communicate with us from time to time, to let us know they were alive and well. Sometimes they even sent a little money. But by that time money was no good anymore. You couldn't buy a thing with it.

And then, one day in January 1945, the Germans went out of Budapest and the Russians came in. Endre and I returned to our apartment and waited for the rest of the family, hoping that they would all be alive. One day—it was the happiest day of lives—Marianne and Pista came. I told them that they should stay with us till everything would be all right. Then my father and his wife came too. He was eighty-two years old but aside from being very thin, he was fit and in good spirits. I think he survived so well because Hilda took such good care of him. Later, we heard from my niece Eva and my nephew Zoltan, and they also came to us. They went to some neighbors to live.

It's funny, but mothers will always be mothers. What was the first thing I saw when my daughter Marianne walked through my door? That she was wearing a pair of Pista's old slacks under her skirt. So the first thing I said to her was, "Oh, Marianne, those pants are so dirty!"

MARIANNE

When we left the air raid shelter of the Swedish consulate, the first place to which Pista and I went was not to his factory in the City Hall building, where I had my jewelry in the safe, but to my parents' apartment on Akafca 6. We knew that if they were alive and well, my parents would be there, waiting for the rest of the family to come and find them. So we picked our way through the ruins and there was the building, Akacfa 6, still standing. The walls were full of bullet holes, and the windows were gone, but my parents' apartment was still there, and so were my parents!

When I walked into the living room I saw, hanging on the wall, the portrait of me that my parents hired an artist to do when I was five or six years old. There were bullet holes in the wall all around the portrait, but the picture and the frame were untouched. Later, we found out that during the siege there'd been soldiers in the apartment; they probably used that wall around my portrait for target practice!

The plumbing was another story. We had no water. We had to bring in the water from wells outside because the water pipes were broken.

There were also two temporary tenants in the apartment; a pair of schoolteachers whom my parents found there when they returned from the "Swedish house." These two women had simply moved into the apartment during the siege to take shelter from the bombs, and they just stayed.

I think the story of our family is one of the great miracles that occurred in Budapest or anywhere else during those days—that an entire Jewish family should be able to return home from hiding and find everyone alive and well. A few days after we came back, my grandfather and his wife came, too. They'd survived in the ghetto. And then came my sister-in-law Klári, her husband, Tibor, and their daughter, Zsuzsi. Eventually, my cousins Eva and Zoltan returned also.

We were all starved. I remember that the first night my parents and we were together, one of the two schoolteachers brought out a loaf of bread! She and her roommate kept it in the kitchen, and then, one by one, everyone else sneaked out into the kitchen when nobody was around, and cut off a little bit of the bread. We hadn't seen bread in a long, long time! We were ashamed to be doing this behind each other's back but in that way, at least, everybody got a little piece of bread that very first night.

As things gradually settled down, we tried to make some sort of life for ourselves. One day Mr. Ágoston, who'd owned the Ujpesti textile plant where Pista first learned the textile business, turned up. He told us he and his wife had no place to stay because the villa they owned in the fashionable part of Buda was still occupied by the Russians. So, Pista and I invited the Ágostons to move in with us temporarily at my parents' apartment. They accepted, and my parents promptly offered them their own big bedroom.

We already had two staple grocery items of which we were very proud: dried onions and dried beans. I don't remember where they came from, whether we got them from neighbors or whether we found them in one of our cupboards. But now there came the problem of cooking. In the middle of one of the rooms we found a little Franklin stove; probably the soldiers had brought it into the apartment during the siege. We now used that stove not only for heat—it was still winter—but also for cooking.

No one in our entire household knew how to cook. Not even Mother—she'd always had someone else to cook our family's meals. So nobody seemed to know what to do with the onions and the beans. In the end, I, the youngest member of the household, was appointed chef. I knew something about cooking because I'd always liked being in the kitchen. I used to sit in the kitchen studying for my *matura* exam, and when I took a few minutes' rest from studying, I'd watch our maid, Lujza, how she did things. Well, now was the time to put my skills to work. My cousin, Eva, tried to help, but she didn't know the first thing about cooking. She put something like a quarter of our sack of dried beans into our soup pot, filled the pot with water and put the pot on the stove. The result was absolute disaster. The dried beans drank up the water very quickly; they swelled and swelled and practically grew out of the pot. I panicked because I was afraid we'd all drown in beans!

The weather was bitter cold and snow fell almost every day, but we went out into the streets each morning to pick up pieces of wood, from doors and windows of bombed-out houses. Some of the wood we used for making a little sled on which we could transport other interesting "finds," things we either could use in our household or barter for food.

We began bartering wood for the necessities of life—doesn't that sound ridiculous? One day my husband came home with a big sack of food. He didn't know what was inside; all he knew was that he'd received it in return for some wooden boards. I looked inside the bag; it was filled with dried mushrooms. This was fantastic! We hadn't seen such a delicacy in a long, long time. There were some brittle strips mixed in with the dried mushrooms that looked to me like noodles. Later on I found out that these strips were not noodles but worms that had died and dried up together with the mushrooms! But I didn't know this when I poured some of the mixture into the soup pot and made a soup out of it. Mr. Ágoston said it was one of the tastiest meals he had ever eaten and that I cooked "like an angel." We had so much of the dried mushroom and "noodle" stuff left over in the sack that we traded half of it with a neighbor for some flour.

Soon Pista and I went into business, after a fashion. On the corner of our apartment building there was a jewelry store. Its owner came back after the siege and found that, miraculously, most of his stock in wrist watches was still there. At about that time it became known all over Budapest that the Russian soldiers were crazy about watches; they called them *chassi*. On the street they'd stop whomever they saw and say, *"Davajchassi,"* which meant, "Give me your watch," and you'd give your watch to them because you never knew whether they wouldn't shoot you if you refused. Well, one day this man who had the jewelry store said to us, "Why don't we start business with the Russian soldiers? Why should we let them get away with stealing watches when we could sell them watches for money, or maybe for barter?" So he gave each of us a couple of watches with which to try our luck. I went out into one of the public squares of the city to show the watches to the passing Russian soldiers. Oh—the Russians just loved them and snapped them up. They were perfectly willing to pay for them—either with cash or with some other article. They didn't try to steal any of the watches from me. They'd roll up the sleeves of their army shirts, cover their arms with wrist watches from wrist to elbows, and show off their loot to everyone they met. But they were really stupid; they didn't know that watches (at least the non-electronic kind in those days) didn't run forever but had to be wound. So whenever one of their watches stopped, they thought it was *kaput.* They'd keep it as an ornament because it looked so nice, but they'd buy—or steal—a new watch that wasn't *kaput* yet.

We also had other contacts with our Russian liberators. All day long, Russian soldiers would knock on our door—or kick the door in, if they felt like it—and ask whether they could use our bathroom to shave. Those who were more "cultured" and friendly would say "thank you" afterwards and offer us small gifts. Those who weren't so considerate—well, it was just tough luck.

There were a lot of women in the Red Army, and they loved brassieres. You have to know that Russian women are built in a peculiar way. They have the most fantastic, huge bosoms. And they thought the more they pushed their breasts up, the better it would look. And so, what watches were for the men, brassieres became for the women. I remember that once, walking through the streets, Pista and I passed a bombed-out department store.

This store had a lot of ladies' hose hanging in the show windows. But the Russian women didn't seem to be interested in the stockings. All they wanted was brassieres.

We waited a few weeks before going to see what was left in the City Hall building of Pista's factory. In the beginning, the downtown section was unsafe, because of the looting and and the debris. But, finally I decided I wanted to know whether the factory was still there, and also what happened to the jewelry I'd left there, in the safe. When Pista and I arrived, the City Hall building was still smoldering. Perhaps a bomb had gone off belatedly, or maybe some looters had set it on fire. We wanted to look for the safe, but because of the fire we couldn't get close to the building. So we stood there a while, waiting for something to happen. After nightfall it began to snow. I wanted to stay on, but Pista said, "We can't stand here all night long, you know! We'll come back early in the morning. By that time the snow should have put the fire out. Then we'll be able to look around for the safe."

My instinct told me not to give up the search so fast, but Pista insisted that we leave, and I left with him—against my own better judgment. When we returned early the next morning, the fire was out. I was about to cross the street and approach the building, when I saw two husky Russian soldiers carrying a kind of slab. On the slab was our own safe! There, right before my eyes, the Russians were taking away the last of my precious possessions! My jewelry had survived the Germans, and the bombings, but now it had fallen into the hands of our liberators! And I couldn't do anything about it because I knew that if I went up to those Red Army men and told them that the safe was mine, they would have taken me along with my safe. That jewelry could have been a great help to us in starting life anew, but—some things simply aren't meant to be.

More and more people we knew reappeared in Budapest. One day, on the street, as I was about to step off the curb, I saw a man sitting on the edge of the curb. By that time I looked somewhat presentable and civilized. I was young—remember, not yet twenty years old—and it's not so hard for women of that age to regain their good looks. Suddenly I heard a man say my name and I looked down at him, sitting on the curb. He stared and stared at me, and after a while he stammered, "Marianne, is that really you? Are you still alive?" I recognized his voice. It was André Romay, a young man, whom I'd known before the war. His original name was Friedmann, but he'd changed it to Romay; it sounded more sophisticated and less Jewish. He'd always been thin, but now he was a mere bundle of skin and bones wrapped in rags. And he looked absolutely desperate. He told me he'd been liberated from the Mauthausen concentration camp in Austria and had walked back from there, in the snow and the cold, all the way to Budapest. He looked at me and said, "Marianne, if you're alive, I think my parents may be alive, too. Just seeing you, so alive and so pretty, gives me the will to go on living. I was ready to sit here till I died, but now I want to get up and go to our old house. Will you please go with me? Maybe I'll find my father and mother there." I accompanied him to his parents' apartment and, sure enough, his parents were there, alive and well! I was happy that, here in Budapest, I was the first person to meet André and restore his will to live.

There were also other happy reunions at my parents' home. One day there was a knock on the door of Akacfá 6. It was my cousin, Irene Szecsi, one of my father's nieces. Before the war she had lived in the countryside. From there she was deported to a concentration camp, together with her two young children. She was so happy to find us alive that she began to hope that, perhaps, her husband and children might be alive also. We invited Irene to stay with us for a while until she could get her strength back and make plans for the future. She told us that her children had been snatched from her at the concentration camp. The last time she had heard from her husband, Armin, it was from a labor camp. Later, she heard that the camp had been liberated by the Russians and that all the inmates who were still alive had been deported to Siberia. Well, Irene stayed with us for the rest of the winter and for part of the next spring. And then, one day, once again, there was a knock on the door of Akacfá 6 and there stood Armin! It was one of the most moving reunions I have ever seen.

It was wonderful that this should have happened at the home of my parents.

Akacfá 6 was the address in Budapest that everyone in the family knew. It was the place where our relatives used to gather before the war because they could always be sure of a warm welcome there. So, perhaps it was only natural that after the war our surviving relatives should come to Akacfá 6 to find out who of the family was still alive.

Mr. and Mrs. Tabák, who permitted me to hide out in their apartment, survived the siege. I went to them to find out what had happened to the perfumes, the lotions and the other cosmetics I'd stored at their air raid shelter. The women I knew were interested in looking beautiful again; I thought that maybe I could start selling them these beauty aids. But Mrs. Tabák told me that Russian soldiers had already helped themselves to everything. Imagine, they drank up the colognes and perfumes like so much liquor!

One day Lujza, out faithful maid, appeared at our house with the gold Marvin watch, my precious graduation gift. When Lujza had left our home, after the law was passed forbidding gentiles to work for Jews as servants, she had taken the watch with her and buried it in the garden of a villa in the suburbs where her sister had been working as a caretaker. Lujza buried the watch under a rose bush and when she went out to look for it after the Germans left, she found it there. And, now she brought it back to me. This was the only piece of jewelry I got back. It remains with me to this day as a souvenir of my girlhood.

Finally, Pista and I gathered up enough courage to visit our apartment in Buda, the apartment we'd lived in during the first weeks of our marriage. The building looked like an elaborate stage setting. One wall was gone, completely blown away by bombs, so you could see all the apartments on that side exposed. We could see our own apartment even from quite a distance. Our furniture was still there, only the curtains were missing. Well, Pista and I thought that was very nice; maybe we could get in somehow and find a few things in the closets or drawers. But one of Pista's gentile friends told me that gentile tenants had moved into the place after we'd left, and they'd cleaned out everything, leaving only the furniture. That was the end of our apartment.

Pista and I realized that we couldn't stay at my parents' place forever, and so we started to look for a place of our own. When we moved, we invited Lujza to stay with us. She had a boyfriend, and he lived with us, too, part of the time. Lujza became pregnant, but the boyfriend couldn't marry her because I think he already had a wife somewhere. When Lujza went into labor, I took her to the hospital. The baby was a boy and I became his godmother. He and Lujza lived with us until we left Budapest. I heard that eventually the boyfriend married Lujza and gave the boy his name. Unfortunately for Lujza, her husband died young. Lujza survived him for many years; she was still alive when I visited Hungary with my daughter Vivian in the 1970s. I went to see her then, and I sent her CARE packages and other gifts until she died. For a while I kept in touch with her son, but then he got married and I never heard from him again.

Meanwhile, at Akacfá 6, my parents were able to breathe more easily. First Pita and I moved out. Then, the Ágostons, who had been living in my parents' big bedroom for months, heard their villa in Buda was no longer occupied by the Russians; so they said good-by to my parents and moved into the villa. Next, my mother-in-law, and Pista's sister and brother-in-law, Klári and Tibor Vayda, moved back to the apartment they'd left when the Germans came. Grandfather and his wife, Hilda, went back to their old apartment. The only homeless relative my parents still had with them was my cousin Eva, whose husband, András hadn't come back. Eva's brother, Zoltan, had a place of his own in Budapest.

Pista went into business in earnest now. Mr. Ágoston opened up a jobber business in kerchiefs and other textiles, and Pista became his representative. They took in a partner, Tibor Waldman, who'd been deported during the war but survived and returned to Budapest. (Today Mr. Waldman is living in the United States, in New York City. He is a successful businessman, and remained a good friend to us.) We made a good living from that business, and life in Budapest could have been very nice for us, but I certainly wanted none of it. Already during the siege, when I divided my time between air-raid shelters and the streets that had turned into a battlefield between the Germans and the Russians, I made up my mind that I, for one, would never stay in Hungary for good, no matter how rich I could become there, and no matter what government would take power. I couldn't see myself rearing children in Europe, where so many of our relatives had lost their lives. By this time we knew that Mother's sister, Rozsi, her husband, Musu and their son, Bandi had been killed. All of Uncle Musu's brothers and sisters were gone, too. The only survivors left from our part of that family were Eva and Zoltan. And Eva, of course, was left without her husband. Mother's former brother-in-law, Feri Ullmann (who'd been married to her sister Csilla) and his second wife, Gizi, and my cousin Luci (the daughter of Feri and Csilla), with whom I'd spent the last summer before the Germans came, were dead also. Except for his nieces Anci and Irene Szecsi, my father's family had been practically wiped out. Irene's husband, Armin, came back from deportation, but their children had perished. Eventually, Irene and Armin settled in Israel and had a new family, but their experiences during the war left them scarred, physically and mentally. And so I had enough, not only of Hungary, but of all of Europe. I was tuned to America, and my only hope was that we'd go to America the first moment we could. I tried to plant the same idea into the head of my husband, Pista.

IV
Primavera

ZOLTAN

In February 1945 my sister Eva and I went to our home in Nyiregyháza, to find out what had become of our home and farm, and to see whether there was anyone who knew anything about our parents and our brother, Bandi.

Of course, we found the house stripped of almost everything. Only the very heavy furniture was still there. We discovered some notes in my father's handwriting; apparently, before he and my mother went to the ghetto, he hid some of the family's jewelry. He wrote something to the effect that he planned to bury a few pieces in the ground. But, that's all we ever learned about the jewelry; it did not turn up anywhere.

In the attic, we discovered a few family pictures. These pictures were all that was left of our immediate family. We met several people who had been in the Nyiregyháza ghetto, and a friend of mine who had returned from Auschwitz. He told Eva and me that he'd been with our father until a certain date; that was all he knew. Many months later, after the war had ended, a cousin of mine, on my father's side, who'd been on the same deportation transport as my parents and Bandi, told me the rest of the story. My mother, he said, had been ordered to move to the left during the "selection." This was the "sorting-out" process the Jews had to undergo as soon as they arrived at a concentration camp. Those who were ordered to move to the right had a chance of temporary survival at hard labor. Those who were told to move to the left were killed at once. That is what happened to my mother. My father, at first, was put to work in a labor detail, but after a while he was put through another "selection," and this time he, too, was ordered to the left. . . .

My brother Bandi went with my parents as far as Auschwitz. In January 1945, when the Russians were coming closer all the time, the Germans evacuated the camp. Bandi was in the last transport of inmates that was taken out of Auschwitz westward, into Germany. A friend of ours came back from Dachau. He told us he had seen Bandi in Dachau, too. Eventually, a cousin of mine, who is now living in Trenton, New Jersey, had to go to Germany to testify at the Nuremberg trials. On his trip, he visited Dachau. And there, in Dachau, my cousin found the official records that the rotten Germans kept. In the records there was a card with Bandi's name, date of birth and date of death. According to these records, my brother died on April 11, 1945, only days before Dachau was liberated.

Eva and I tried to salvage what was left of our lives. My textile mill in Budapest was in ruins. My gentile partner, Ervin Stojko-vitz, had disappeared—who knows where? So I went to Szabolcs-baka, near Nyiregyháza, where we had our farm. I wanted to see what "Aryan" had stolen it after my parents left, and whether, as my parents' heirs, I could get it back. After some legal proceed-ings, I got back the farm, but my satisfaction lasted for only a few days, because then the Communists took over in Hungary, and I was left with just a token measure of land, the maximum that the Communists allowed any individual to own.

I had plenty of troubles on the farm under the Communists. They said that since I obviously couldn't work the whole farm alone, with my own two hands, they'd take over the place and divide the property rights among the peasants. But at that time the Communists weren't entirely in the driver's seat as yet, so I managed to get around the law and hired a pair of horses, a tractor, and two or three local farmhands. It was lucky I could get these people to work for me because I really wasn't familiar with farming, and, frankly, I wasn't interested in it.

So, for a while, I made some sort of living from the farm and

divided my time between Szabolcsbaka, Nyíregyháza and Budapest, where my sister Eva was still living with Aunt Aranka.

But in 1948 the Communists became very strict about the rights
of landowners. They wanted to liquidate the small landowners—
kulaks, they called them. So they passed a law that all the fields
of every privately-owned farm in Hungary had to be harvested
completely by a certain date. If you didn't meet the deadline, you
were liable to severe punishment. But how was I to harvest my
field? By that time I didn't have the tractor anymore, not even the
horses, because the Communists had taken everything away.

Luckily, Szabolcsbaka was a small place and I had some good
friends there, including the Communist party secretary, a gentile
by the name of . . . I shall call J. I heard that during the Hitler
period J. did a lot of favors for Jewish boys in labor camps; after
all, the Nazis had been the enemies of the Communists just as
much as they'd been the enemies of the Jews. Luckily, during the
period after the war, I was in a position to help him, so that he
became obligated to me. Although he was the Communist party
secretary for the entire district, he and his family were starving
because these party hacks didn't get paid. So, I sent him food from
my farm every day—at night, under cover of darkness, so nobody
should see. J. told me he was heartbroken at the thought of having
to accept food from a bourgeois. No matter how nice I might be
as an individual, I was officially an enemy of the working class.
J. was a one hundred percent idealistic Communist. However, his
family was starving. So, he said, as long as nobody in town knew
about it, he would accept food from my farm, and he hoped that
someday he'd be able to repay my kindness.

Well, that "someday" came sooner than either he or I expected.
One day I was picked up by the police and taken to police
headquarters. I asked someone to send for "Comrade J." because
I was in trouble. An hour later, in my cell, I could hear J. yelling
outside, "What's going on here? Who picked up this man? For
what reason?" And so on, and so on. And then he yelled, "Release
this man at once! Let him go home!" And so I was a free man
again.

The next morning a friend of mine, a Jewish fellow who was

a member of the Communist party, came to the farm with a message from Mr. J.: "Comrade J. stuck out his neck for you yesterday because you really helped him, but unfortunately he won't be able to do anything for you in the future because he can't afford to jeopardize his position."

I understood only too well. That same day I went to Budapest and started to work on ways of leaving Hungary. This was, as I've said, in 1948. The borders were already sealed off; you couldn't get into Hungary, or out of the country, except with official papers. Since I was in no position to obtain official papers, I had to fake them. I made contact with some very resourceful people, who gave me good advice. They told me about a place where, for five hundred American dollars or half a kilo of gold, you could get papers identifying you as a Rumanian refugee traveling through Hungary on the way to Rumania. These papers, transit visas bearing the seal of the Rumanian government, were valid for only 48 hours, but you could use them to leave Hungary, even if you were not going to Rumania but to Austria. I managed to get such papers for myself and for my sister, Eva. Eva needed two additional sets of documents, because by that time she had remarried. Her first son, Andy (named after our brother Bandi), was already six months old. I got my hands on the money we needed for the papers, and I obtained the papers for all of us, complete with faked Rumanian names.

And so Eva, her husband Martin Korda, and their son Andy and I boarded a train for Austria. We had heard that once you got into the American zone of Austria, you had a chance of being allowed to go to the United States as a "displaced person." My cousin Marianne and her husband had arrived in New York two years earlier.

Everything went well until our train stopped at Sopron, the border station between Hungary and Austria. All the passengers were asked to show their papers. Much to our misfortune, the officials felt there was something suspicious about our documents. So, Eva, Martin, little Andy and I were taken off the train. Several couples, and one pregnant woman traveling with a little boy, were also taken off the train. They had no papers at all, not even faked ones. I could see that the pregnant woman was very religious; she wore a traditional, matronly-looking *sheitel*. She came over to me and asked me to help her. "I see that you are a single man," she said. "No wife with you. I also saw that you have some papers. Could you pretend to be my husband?" All right, I agreed. It was, after all, a *mitzvah* to help this unfortunate woman. So I stayed with her when they put us on a truck to take us to the local AVD headquarters. AVD was the Hungarian Communist State Police, the same as the KGB in Russia.

The AVD men started going through our papers and our baggage, which, of course, wasn't much for any of us refugees. All the baggage I had with me was a satchel, which contained a shirt, maybe a pair of socks but, most important, my *tallith* and *tefillin*, which I had used for prayers every day, even during the worst hours of the siege of Budapest.

The AVD man picked my *tallith* and *tefillin* from my satchel. "You mean you were going to take these along with you?" he wanted to know.

"Yes," I replied.

"Very nice," he said, "You may go now." He must have been a Jewish boy with a little spark of Judaism still in his heart, not bitter against Jewishness, like so many other Communists. At any rate, I was allowed to cross the border, into freedom, and so were Eva and her family.

Once I was in Vienna, I made straight for the American consulate. I should add here that back in Budapest, before the Communists took over in Hungary, I got a Hungarian passport (it cost me 150 American dollars). With that passport, I went to the American consulate in Budapest and applied for an American immigration visa. I got the visa, but the Communists took away my passport. I went back to the American consulate in Budapest and told them my sad story: How would I get to the United States now that my passport, with the American visa stamped into it, was gone? The people at the consulate said not to worry. As long as I had an American visa, I could report to any American consulate, anywhere in the world, and they would contact the American consulate in Budapest to verify my visa.

So, I now went to the American consulate in Vienna and told my story to an official there. At first the man tried to make things difficult for me. When I told him I had no official identification papers (I had only the faked Rumanian papers, with a faked name) he said he had no reason to believe that I was really Zoltan Weiss and that I had really received an American visa from the consulate in Budapest. But eventually, I was able to convince him that I'd told him the truth. He asked me where I was staying in Vienna, and promised to let me know as soon as he had word from Budapest.

I stayed in Vienna for about five months after that. Eva, Martin, Andy and I shared one hotel room in Vienna. Later, when the Kordas moved to a displaced persons' camp in Salzburg, I stayed in the hotel room by myself. Later, I moved into the Rothschild "hotel." Before the war, this had been Vienna's Jewish hospital. Now it served as a shelter for Jewish displaced persons, with free room and board (the food was kosher, and very good) and even a couple of pennies' spending money. For entertainment, we refugees at the Rothschild "hotel" played cards. But I didn't spend all my time playing cards, waiting for my papers or for opportunities to make money on the black market. I went back to the textile school where I'd studied before the war and took some private lessons in textile design. I thought this would be a good way of earning money once I was in the United States.

One day, early in the summer of 1949, I received a card from the American consulate telling me that my papers had arrived and that I should come to call for them. Unfortunately, it was a "false alarm." The papers were for another man named Zoltan Weiss, not me.

Meanwhile, my affidavit expired. In those days, if you wanted an immigration visa for the United States, you had to present an affidavit—a document from an American citizen promising that, as long as you had no other means of financial support, this American citizen would take the responsibility of helping you so that you wouldn't become dependent on public welfare. I had received such an affidavit from our cousin Charles Zucker in New York. But, now this affidavit had expired. It looked as if my visa, the one I received in Budapest, would also expire, and that might well have been the end of my American dream. However, Charlie was nice enough to send me a new affidavit and in August 1949, six weeks after the "false alarm," my papers finally came through.

By that time I had used up most of my money, so the American Jewish Joint Distribution Committee (we refugees called it the "Joint" before we knew its real full name) paid for my boat ticket. My boat was due to sail from a seaport on the French Riviera, near Nice. A number of other refugees from Vienna were to sail for America on the same boat. Now the problem was, how were we to get to France from Vienna? We couldn't leave Vienna by train because the area outside the city through which we would have had to pass was occupied by the Russians. So, the "Joint" had to fly us out of Vienna by plane. Our first stop was Munich. There, we were given train tickets, and another train, for our "port of embarkation."

I still remember the name of the boat. It was a Polish ship, the SS *Sobieski*. I also remember very clearly the day we landed in New York: it was September 12, 1949, only a few days before Rosh Hashanah, the Jewish New Year.

My sister Eva and her family had no American visas. So they attempted to get into the United States by roundabout means. Before they left Budapest, they bought visas for Cuba. If you had a Cuban visa you could get an American transit visa allowing you to pass through the United States because in those days there were no direct flights or boats from Europe to Havana. In that way, some refugees with American visas (especially if they had relatives or friends in the U.S.A.) managed to stay in America long enough to finagle an American immigration visa. Then they could forget about Cuba and settle in the United States unfortunately, when the Kordas left Budapest, a new government took over in Cuba, and the Cuban visas were canceled. This meant no American transit visas for the Kordas. Luckily, later, in Salzburg, they were able to get visas for Canada, where the immigration laws were not strict as in the United States. And so, they were able to leave Europe a few days after me, on a displaced persons' boat, which took them to Halifax. From there, Eva, Martin and Andy went to Toronto, where they still live today.

Meanwhile, I settled in New York. There, I met Helen, a girl from Slovakia who'd been through all the concentration camps. First she was in Auschwitz. After that, she was in Dachau, then back in Auschwitz again, then in Sachsenhausen, and finally in Bergen-Belsen, where she and her sister were liberated. From Bergen-Belsen, the Red Cross took her to Sweden, on a Red Cross boat. At the time, Sweden took in many girls like Helen, who had survived the death camps, were all alone in the world and had to be nursed back to health before they could make any plans for their future. Helen was placed into a hospital in Göteborg; after that, she spent some time in a quarantine camp. Finally, she was placed with a Swedish gentile family, also in Göteborg. To pay for her room and board, she went to work in a textile factory. Little did she know then that she would marry into a "textile family"! She stayed in Göteborg for two years. Then, an uncle in the United States sent her American papers. That is how Helen came to New York, and that is how we met and married.

I established myself in the field I knew best—textile design. I specialized in Jacquard designs, meaning that the design is not applied to the material but woven into the material itself.

Helen and I have two children, Rosalyn and Murray. Rosalyn is married in Flatbush—a nice residential neighborhood in Brooklyn. Murray is an actuary; he was just married and is about to settle in Israel with his bride.

Helen and I live in Queens, in a pleasant Jewish neighborhood. We are not among those people who never talk about what we went through in Hungary. We never kept our experiences from our children. Also, each year, on the 26th day of Nissan Holocaust Memorial Day, we attend special services with our children at the Young Israel of Forest Hills. There, the survivors gather, together with any Jews who were born and raised in this country, to remember the past and to pray that no future generation of Jews will ever have to endure what we suffered forty years ago.

EVA

When the war ended, my brother Zoltan and I learned that our parents had been killed in Auschwitz, and that our brother Bandi had perished in Dachau.

All I knew then about András—the husband with whom I had lived only a few days—was that somebody had seen him somewhere in Buchenwald.

All our other relatives and friends who had stayed with my aunt Aranka and uncle Endre Lowy during the siege had returned to their own homes, or moved into new ones. But, here I was, still with the Lowys, in their apartment on Akafca 6. Uncle Endre and Aunt Aranka were worried about me and my future. Everything was done to find out whether, by some miracle, András had survived. Finally, we located the records of Buchenwald, and there I found out for sure that I was a widow. András had been shot by the Germans late in February 1945.

My uncle Endre was a wonderful man, a very kindhearted human being who loved to do good deeds, including matchmaking. One day when Zoltan and I were in the country, a gentleman came to him for some business and personal advice. His name, he said, was Martin Korda. Uncle Endre asked him whether his family survived the war. Martin replied that his wife Lili Szèkely had been pregnant with their first child when she was deported. They'd married in 1944, just like András and I, but Martin's wife Lili was shot because she could not take the long march out of the country toward Austria in the late fall of 1944. Her young sister who was with her jumped to her rescue and was shot as well. Another horror story!

"I have a *shidduch* for you," my matchmaking uncle spoke up, "my wife's niece. She isn't in Budapest just now. She and her brother are in Nyiregyháza to see what happened to the home and the property of their parents. But she will be back in Budapest next week. May I invite you to our home to meet her then?" And so, Martin Korda and I met, and eventually we were married.

After our marriage, we decided that we didn't want to live in Hungary anymore—not after what had happened to our family. I was pregnant, and I said to Martin that I didn't want to have my baby in Hungary, where neither I nor my family were wanted. Faced with the problems of migration, Martin was slow to agree with what was inevitable; but after careful thought, he said yes.

Our first choice was the United States, where Marianne and her husband Pista went in 1947. But only Zoltan was lucky enough to get an American visa. Martin and I couldn't. So we devised a different plan. We got our Cuban visas stamped into our passports. But then, from one day to the next, there was a change of government in Cuba, and we lost not only our Cuban visas, but our Hungarian passports as well.

So, we remained in Hungary and our first son, Andy, was born there. When Andy was five months old, we left Hungary for Austria together with my brother Zoltan. We spent six months in Austria, looking for some country in the free world that would let us in. Finally, we got immigration visas for Canada, and we left Europe only a few days after Zoltan sailed for New York. Our boat landed in Quebec. From there we went to Toronto. Toronto was where we settled, where our second son, Jeffrey, was born in 1952 and where all of us still live today. Andy is a doctor; he has one son, Ryan. Jeffrey is an artist and gemologist.

Marianne's daughter, Vivian, who was born in New York, is living in Toronto also. She and I have one great interest in common. Both of us are artists. I work at painting, printmaking, graphic arts and sculpture. One of my favorite sculptures—it's now at Marianne's home in Columbus—is one I've called Primavera. It symbolizes rebirth, a new life. In the beginning, I must admit, I wasn't able to face life with such optimism. When you have lost your parents, your brother, a young husband, and many dozens of relatives in the Holocaust, it's hard to be an optimist. But basically, though I may look delicate, I am a strong person. And as the months and years went by, and it became obvious that whoever had survived and had returned, and that those who had not returned could not possibly be alive any longer, I was eager to get on with a new life, a life of my own. I wanted a husband, children—a family. I have acquired all this, and now I truly feel that my own outlook is in character with my *Primavera*. I am able to look to the future without bitterness or fear.

VICTOR

He believes that many artists who survived the Holocaust and were able to build normal, healthy lives afterwards were helped tremendously by their ability to express their emotions through their art. He thinks this was true in his case although he wasn't able to make a living from his art when he first arrived in the United States in 1946.

The first months following the liberation of Budapest were very difficult. He had been safe during the siege, working as the telephone operator in the Swedish consulate, where Marianne and Pista Reiss, among many, many others, were hidden. His parents were able to stay in their own home in Budapest, because his mother was gentile, but his parents were constantly harassed by the police, who kept searching the apartment—probably to see whether his parents were giving shelter to Jews. The searches, and then the siege, with all the bombing and shelling, the hunger and the fear of death, proved too much for his father, who had a heart condition. Although he lived to see Budapest liberated, his father died a few weeks later at the age of fifty-six. His mother survived. He brought her to America, and she lived to the age of eighty-four.

Just before he left Budapest, he married his wife, Eva. She was a survivor of Auschwitz. He met Eva by accident, when he went to the home of one of his girlfriends to see whether she had survived. It turned out that she had been in Auschwitz and had met Eva there. The two girls had become very close friends. Eva's entire family had been killed, and so this girlfriend invited Eva to stay with her.

When Eva and Victor landed in New York, all they had was five dollars that they'd been given by the "Joint"—the American Jewish Joint Distribution Committee. During his first six months in the United States he couldn't work as a violinist because the unions didn't admit anyone who'd been living in the United States less than half a year. Eva got a job selling neckties in a Fifth Avenue store, for $25.00 a week, which was not much in 1946. This was their only income for quite a while. Yet, he says, "in all honesty, we never lost faith for a minute, I never felt even a moment of despair. I can truthfully say that Eva and I had some wonderful, happy times on those $25.00 per week."

His first job took him away from New York. It was with the Pittsburgh Symphony Orchestra, under Dr. Fritz Reiner. But, he missed New York, so he auditioned for Radio City Music Hall and was hired as concertmaster there. Later, he became concert-master of the Metropolitan Opera House orchestra; he held that job for six years. Then, Dr. Reiner took over as conductor of the Chicago Symphony Orchestra and invited Victor Aitay to come as co-concertmaster. That was 27 years ago, and that's where he is yet.

In addition to his work with the Chicago Symphony, he is in the Chicago String Quartet; the four musicians have been playing together for the past 20 years. They give about 50 concerts a year in the United States, in South America, and all over Europe. They enjoy this very much because it gives them an outlet of musical experiences in addition to the symphony playing. He thinks that it lends an added dimension to their music making because they approach the music from a different standpoint: "not in accordance with the wishes of a conductor but with our own individual tastes and emotions that come through when we play a quartet."

In the summer he plays at the Ravinia Festivals, and also as-sumes the role of conductor. He conducts the Lake Forest Sym-phony, which gives him great satisfaction, "because I happen to think that conducting is really the ultimate in music-making. I love to play the violin, I love to play quartet, I love to teach, but the ultimate achievement really is to conduct an orchestra, and to convey your own wishes to your orchestra—and to your audience. I think this is the supreme goal of any musician."

He has never had a desire to visit Budapest, or Hungary. His mother went back to Budapest once—to visit his father's grave in the Jewish cemetery. But, she couldn't find the grave. Since Victor had paid the government for 50 years of perpetual care, his mother went to the cemetery office to find the record, because she knew exactly where the grave should have been. She examined the record, but she couldn't even find a record of the grave. When she demanded to know what happened to her husband's grave, she was told that they needed the space for a prominent Communist party member who had died.

Because of this, Victor could never bring himself to visit Hungary. Several times he considered going, but as yet he hasn't.

KLÁRI

When my husband, Tibor, arrived at his sister-in-law's apartment on Jozsika Street, where our little daughter Zsuzsi and I had been hiding, he promptly fainted. Despite the pieces of shrapnel in his knee, he had somehow made it to Jozsika Street, on all fours, by sheer willpower. But once he was with us, inside the apartment, his strength gave out.

The Germans were gone and I wanted to return to our own home, but Tibor was in no condition to go. So we stayed with him on Jozsika Street for another few days. Then we said good-bye to our sister-in-law Gizi and started on our way. You can't imagine what that walk was like—my little Zsuzsi hanging on to my one hand, while I tried to keep Tibor on his feet with my other hand, and all three of us trying to avoid tripping over the debris, the dead horses, and human bodies that littered the street!

Finally we arrived at our apartment building, Csáky utca 15. The windows of our apartment were broken, another family was living there. They agreed to move out, but I couldn't imagine how we could turn this back into our nice and friendly little home again. Still, we tried, and we settled down again, to a halfway normal life, for eleven years, until the Hungarian Revolution of 1956.

On November 24, 1956, very early, on a snowy, slippery morning, Tibor and I and our children—Zsuzsi by then had a little brother, Tomas—closed the door of our apartment behind us. We left everything there, except that each of us carried one small bag with our essential possessions. We left our home with a prayer in our hearts that God might help us through all the perils ahead, and that we would be reunited with my brother Pista and his family in the United States.

Pista and his wife, Marianne, had left for the United States earlier, in 1947. They already had two American children—Ronnie, who was born the year they came to New York, and Vivian, who was born in 1952. Marianne's mother, Aranka, was also in New York by then. Pista had tried to build a new life in Budapest; he wasn't doing too badly in business, despite the Communists. But he and Marianne couldn't see themselves spending the rest of their days in a country where Communists ruled supreme. Pista, who was always a devoted son and brother—our mother died in Budapest in 1952—sent us papers for America several times before the revolution, but nobody was allowed to leave Hungary then.

The revolution began on October 23, 1956, and one month later, almost to the day, we escaped. We crossed the border into Austria. In Vienna we heard that it would be almost impossible for us to enter the United States in the near future. We were glad when Canada accepted us.

Eventually, a little while later, we managed to enter the United States after all. We settled in Los Angeles, where Tibor and I went into business. You might say we were art dealers, working mostly with paintings.

We are plain, quiet citizens. Our only claim to fame is our daughter Zsuzsi's short period as a movie star. She adopted the movie name Valerie Varda, but now she is a happily married Mrs. Susanne Sobel. Our son, Tomas, is a professor of mathematics at the University of California.

Tibor and I are getting on in years, and so we retired from business. I think we have made a good life for ourselves, and nothing gives us more happiness than to share our time with our children and two grandchildren. We see them almost every day.

PAULINE

Soon after the end of the war—I think it was in September 1945 —my late husband, Nathan, and I paid a visit to Europe. Nathan's chief purpose in making the trip was to go to Hungary, to see his great-uncle Henrick Zucker and to find out what he could do to help the other relatives.

Our first stop in Europe was Paris; from there, we went to Vienna. In order to enter Hungary from Austria then, you needed a certain pass—I think they called it a "gray ticket." Nathan received the pass but I did not. So we agreed that he would go to Hungary alone for a few days and I would wait for him in Vienna. We agreed that Nathan would telephone me from Budapest the following day at our hotel, the Hotel Königsberg.

When he failed to call me, I got worried. I tried to put in a call to Budapest, to Uncle Henrick's residence, and to the Lowys, but I could not get through anywhere. I was now really upset. I went to the American consulate, showed the consul my American passport and told him my story. I asked the consul whether he himself could try to put in a call to Budapest. I assured him that I would pay for it, whatever it would cost.

In retrospect, I must say I was very naive! The consul apparently thought so, too. "What's the matter with you people back in the United States?" he wanted to know. "Don't you read the papers? Don't you know what's going on? How did your husband even dare to make a trip like this?" But when he saw how upset I was, he tried to calm me down. "My dear lady," he said. "Compose yourself! Keep calm. We'll try to find out what happened to your husband. We have our ways of doing that, without drawing too much attention to him. Go back to your hotel and wait. Do *not* try to call Budapest again. If you do receive a call from your husband, let us know at once. And if we make contact with him, we'll get in touch with you immediately."

Well, God was good to us. Three days later Nathan turned up in Vienna. He hadn't been able to call me because his calls from Budapest to Vienna—like mine from Vienna to Budapest—were not put through. He didn't have any trouble in Budapest, but he felt that he was being shadowed all the time. And he saw how terrified the Jews in Budapest were about making contact with Americans. Yet some of them took the chance because they hoped the visitors from America would be able to help them, or their relatives. So, when it became known that Nathan was in Budapest, visiting his uncle, a Jewish family—not at all related to us —came to see him. They told him that their son had managed to escape from Hungary by train, holding on to the underside of a freight car! He was lucky; he made it to Vienna and from there to Paris. Now he wanted to go on to Palestine. But all he had was the clothes on his back. The parents knew that Nathan was planning to stop in Paris again on his way back to America. Could he take along with him a suit for their son to give to him in Paris? Of course Nathan agreed. He even offered to visit them at their home and pick up the suit. But the parents said, "No! We can't possibly allow you to take that risk, Herr Zucker! Who knows what will happen to you if somebody sees you walking out of our house with a package under your arm?" And so the father came to the hotel where Nathan was staying. "Well, where's the package?" Nathan asked him. Instead of replying, the father took off his suit! He was wearing two suits, one on top of the other. The suit he'd taken off was for his son in Paris. Nathan put it into his suitcase.

Before Nathan could return to Vienna, he had another visitor, a man named Eisler, whose son and daughter-in-law had also escaped from Hungary and were now in Vienna, waiting for an opportunity to go to Palestine. Mr. Eisler wanted to know whether Nathan would be willing to take some money—American dollars—to the young people. They would need the money for the journey to Palestine. Again, Nathan agreed to help.

As soon as he was back in Vienna, Nathan went to the Rothschild Hospital, where the young Eislers were staying along with hundreds of other displaced persons. The hospital had become a makeshift shelter for refugees. Nathan found the young couple there, and the next day we took them to the kosher restaurant for a good meal. After we'd eaten, Nathan told the Eislers about the money from his parents in Budapest, and wanted to give it to him then and there. But young Mr. Eisler turned ashen pale. "Don't do that here!" he whispered in a strained voice. "But I don't understand. . . ." said Nathan. "You're not in Hungary anymore. You're in Vienna. You don't have to be afraid of anything or anybody here." But the Eislers kept saying, "The walls have ears, you know." So Nathan said to me, "Pauline, you have enough money in your handbag. Take Mrs. Eisler to the ladies' room and settle the business there!" So I took the young woman to the ladies room, and she rolled up the bills into a handkerchief and stuffed them under her girdle! And then we walked the Eislers all the way back to the Rothschild Hospital so they shouldn't be afraid.

On the way we passed the Russian occupied Grand Hotel, and those poor people almost turned to stone, overcome with fright least they be stopped. As they had no papers, they told us that they would have been shot on the spot. As an American, I had a hard time relating to this reality.

CHARLES

I didn't visit Hungary until December 1946, over a year after my brother Nathan went. I always had great respect for my great-uncle Henrick Zucker and longed to see him again. But I couldn't get a Hungarian visa in New York; you could get that only in Austria. So, like my brother, I made my itinerary Paris—Vienna —Budapest. When I arrived in Vienna I found out it was impossible to get a visa to Hungary. When I let my Hungarian relatives know we wanted to come anyhow they sent me a message that they'd have somebody meet us at a certain place on the Austro-Hungarian frontier with my visa. Of course this was done secretly, in a kind of code, so that nobody should become suspicious.

I had with me another "tourist," my brother-in-law Jack Friedman, my sister's husband, who was an American citizen. Because he was in the diamond business, he spent most of his time traveling back and forth between Belgium and France.

I took with me two valises with things I thought the family might need. At the frontier, we were met, just as my relatives said we would be. I'm an old man and I don't remember things so clearly anymore, but I think that the man who met me was Pista Reiss, Marianne's husband. There were no visas. Instead, he took my valises and said, "Follow me." And so he led us across the border into Hungary. Our first stop was a farmhouse. Suddenly, we heard a sound like from a whistle. Pista whispered to me, "Lie down!" The Communists sent a dog after us, but we ran—Pista ahead of us, with my bags—and we made it into Hungary. If I had known the trouble I'd have, I wouldn't have done it even for $100,000! The way back to Vienna was easier. I did it the legal way—as an American citizen, with the help of the American consulate.

But once we arrived in Budapest, I felt better and I could almost say I had a nice time there. I was so happy to see all my relatives again—my Uncle Henrick, his daughter Aranka and her husband, Marianne, Eva, and all the others! I was only sad that Rozsi and her husband and their son Bandi and all the others were gone. . . .

Once I was with my relatives, I didn't talk in riddles. I was quite open with them. I told them that if they needed affidavits from America, brother Nathan and I would take care of it. We'd also be glad to pay their passage to New York.

I remember New Year's Eve in Budapest. Jack and I spent the evening with Marianne and Pista. A wonderful young couple! We had no hint of their plans to leave, or we would meet again soon, in Paris.

My brother Nathan and I did everything we could to help our relatives leave Europe, such as sending them affidavits. The only one who refused *all* help was my Uncle Henrick. He said that he and his wife, Hilda, were too old to make the trip and settle in the United States. So he and Hilda stayed on in Hungary even after his daughter Aranka and all his surviving grandchildren left. Uncle Henrick died in Budapest in 1949—eighty-six years old. Hilda, his second wife, who was much younger, lived twenty-seven years longer. She died, also in Budapest, in 1976.

MARIANNE

Our American Zucker relatives, Nathan and Charles—and their wives, Pauline and Lottie—were wonderful. As soon as they found out that we had survived, they sent us CARE packages. Pauline sent us clothes, beautiful things that I was able to wear without much alteration. The Zuckers also sent us food. Some of it was strange and unfamiliar. There were cans labeled "Crisco." We thought it was some kind of spread; we had no idea that it was meant for cooking. Then came boxes labeled "Kellogg's Corn Flakes." We thought these corn flakes were meant to be eaten with cocktails, like peanuts. We didn't know it was a break-fast food. The only "cereals" we'd ever known was farina, or oatmeal, and that was eaten hot, usually boiled in milk and sea-soned with sugar and maybe cinnamon. Mostly, you gave that to children, or to sick people. But cold cereal—who'd ever heard of that?

Before long we got our first ten-dollar bill from the United States. One day a man turned up at our apartment and introduced himself as Adrian Heller. He said he'd been born in Hungary but he was now living in the United States. He was in Budapest on the staff of the American military mission. He told us that some-body—he wouldn't say who—had written him our address and told him to give us the ten dollars. Really, by that time we didn't need the money anymore, because Pista was doing very well in the kerchief business with Mr. Agoston and Tibor Waldman, but it was nice to know that someone in America was thinking about us.

All this time Pista was keeping his eyes open for an opportunity to go to the United States. The Zucker brothers in New York assured us they'd be happy to give us affidavits. But it didn't help. The immigration quotas were filled. We could see only one way for us to get to the United States, and that was by obtaining an immigration visa from a country which you could reach only by passing through the U.S.A. My cousin Eva, two years later, along with many others, wanted to obtain immigration visas for Cuba so that they could get transit visas to pass through the United States. Pista and I had decided on Australia. If you had an Australian immigration visa, it was the same as if you had one from Cuba. You could leave Hungary and enter Austria. And since, at that time, the easiest and in fact the only possible way of getting to Australia—or to Cuba—from Europe was by way of the United States, the American government was willing to give you a transit visa, which entitled you to travel through the United States on your way. Once you were in the United States . . . well, we thought we might be able to find a way of staying in America for good and never mind going on to Australia. Or maybe we'd stay in Australia for a while and then try to re-enter the United States from there, as legal immigrants.

In order to get an Australian visa, you had to find someone in Australia to put up a kind of financial guarantee for you, to make sure you wouldn't ask for charity there. At that time, the amount was $2,000. We had friends in Australia who were willing to do this for us. They were Mr. and Mrs. Safrany, who'd gone to Australia from Hungary before the war. We made it clear to them that we had money and would be able to repay them the $2,000 as soon as we arrived to the free world.

After we had our Australian immigration visas—and our American transit visas—I started to plan and prepare for our long trip. Business in Budapest was booming then, because the Communists weren't completely in charge yet. But the money we made wasn't worth much because there was a wild inflation. We'd run to the bank every day with whole satchels full of money but the next day there'd be a devaluation and the money was worth that much less. So I wanted to convert the money into goods we'd be able to use, or to sell, either in Australia or in America.

We knew that we could send household goods to Australia in lift vans—huge crates, maybe as big as a whole room, filled with furniture and household goods. You could send the lift vans ahead of you and have them stored somewhere until you yourself arrived. There were some wonderful silversmiths in Budapest who had started to work again after the war. And if you knew one of them, they'd send you to others also. So, Pista and I began to invest our cash in silver goods—trays, bowls, tea sets, of all sizes and designs, absolutely beautiful. The silversmith packed the articles for us and, to avoid suspicion, we sent them with others overseas. This way even before we left Hungary, we would have enough silver in the United States to sell and convert into cash again, for our living expenses, and to start out in business wherever we would eventually settle.

We decided not to take our heavy furniture with us. Instead, we wanted to sell our apartment, along with all the furniture, to a family who didn't plan on leaving Hungary. We found such a family—they were in the jewelry business and said they had no intention of leaving the country. They took over our apartment, lock, stock and barrel, with everything in it. Much later, we found out that these people had left Hungary after all, for Canada. They put all the furniture in a lift van, and now they are in Canada, living in a place full of our furniture from Budapest . . . It was an odd feeling when I saw it there.

In December 1946, our cousin Charlie Zucker came to Hungary to visit the family. (His brother Nathan had come the year before, soon after the war ended.) Charlie was very happy to see my grandfather, my parents, and Pista and me. We had some very nice times with him in Budapest. His brother-in-law, Jack Friedman, a diamond dealer from New York, came with him. All of us spent New Year's Eve together.

Two days later, on January 2, 1947, secretly, with only a word to our immediate family, Pista and I left Budapest. We took with us a couple of suitcases containing one huge Hungarian salami and generous supply of chocolate bars—oh, yes, and lots of clothes for us! Who knew when we be able to afford new ones again? I did not take any jewelry with me. In those days the searches at the borders were very strict and we didn't want to get into trouble.

Our first stop was in Vienna, which was then still occupied by British, French, American, and Russian troops. The foreign troops didn't really leave Vienna until 1955. In order to be able to pass between the four "occupation sections" of Vienna, you had to have a *rosa Pass*— a "pink slip."

I remember that when we arrived in Vienna it was evening and pitch dark. The city was in ruins and there was a terrible shortage of electric power. Everything was still very much upset from the war. I remember that Pista and I visited the café of the famous Hotel Sacher. I'd always heard in my childhood what a beautiful, elegant place the Sacher was, and how kings and princes from all over the world used to come there incognito to enjoy the gourmet food—and often a girlfriend on the side. But now all that they could serve us at the Sacher was a cup of *ersatz* coffee with soybean milk in it—without sugar, of course.

We had to spend a whole day running around to get the *rosa Pass* and various other papers we would need for the rest of our journey to Australia. Since we didn't want to stay in Vienna any longer than it would take for us to obtain our papers, we did not look for a hotel—in fact, there was no such thing worthy of the name in Vienna then. Instead, we hired a taxi that became our hotel for the day. In return for our Hungarian salami and chocolate bars which I dangled in front of him, for his hungry family at home, the taxi driver took us around the city all day long, waiting for us outside the offices to which we had to go for our documents.

We were able to assemble all the papers we needed in that one day, and that very night we boarded the Arlberg Express for the next lap of our journey—to Paris. It was January and bitter cold, but the Arlberg Express, which was a luxury train before the war, didn't even have heat in the compartments. There was some water dripping from pipes that ran through our compartment, and that water promptly froze. When Pista and I lay down on the seat of our compartment to sleep, Pista's alligator wallet had slipped out of his pocket. When we found the wallet in between the upholstery the next morning it was frozen inside a block of ice. We kept the wallet as a souvenir for a long time.

As our train passed through Europe, stopping at various smaller depots, there was a Swiss stop. There were people in the station selling oranges and bananas to the passengers. I hadn't seen such delicacies in a very long time, and I got off to buy some. Maybe it was childish of me, but later, passing through Germany, as the train pulled out of a station I opened the window of our compartment and threw out my banana and orange peels at hungry-looking Germans who were standing near the tracks, watching the train go by. As I said, it may have been infantile, but sometimes revenge is sweet. . . .

Paris still bore the scars of the war years. I remember that there was a shortage of soap and candles. I needed candles to light on Friday night, but couldn't find candles in any store. Now, no matter where I'd been since the Germans marched into Budapest —in hiding at the Tabàks' for at the Swedish consulate—I had always lit my Sabbath candles, and I wasn't going to break that custom now. As a last resort, I got the idea of going to the Notre Dame Cathedral. They had hundreds of votive candles there flickering around the altars. I picked out two of those candles from a box and took them back with me to our hotel, and so I recited the Sabbath candle blessing over tapers that had been meant to *memorialize* some Christian saint!

When we arrived in Paris, Charlie Zucker was there also, on his way back to New York, and we spent a beautiful evening together. Paris still had a few luxuries to offer, provided you were willing to spend the money. Charlie took us to the Sheherezade, one of the finest restaurants left in town. Then we went on to the Tabarin, one of the best-known night clubs in Paris, where they had the most fantastic floor show, bodies painted with gilt color, doing all kinds of intricate acrobatics.

I had everything. By the time we left Budapest, we were already, as I have told you, very well settled. So I had bought the most magnificent clothing. I was ready for anything and everything. First of all, I had beautiful lingerie made. It was all of pure silk and laces. Everything had been made to order for me by a place that was very famous for made-to-order underwear.

Ready-to-wear, you know, is an American thing. In Hungary everybody who bought clothes had them made. Maybe they have now ready-to-wear things, but not at that time. Anyhow, there were materials available. People brought in silks and wools or whatever was needed, and don't forget my husband was in that type of business. As a matter of fact, he made a trip to Switzerland, I think before we went out, I think he arrived—yes, he made a trip to Switzerland for some business reasons and he brought back beautiful fabrics that were made for the whole family for his-and-hers outfits, my sister-in-law, the children, us. Everybody had just magnificent clothes. And shoes were made, there were marvelous shoemakers to make shoes. At that time all the lizards was very fashionable, just like now.

I had this absolutely fabulous wardrobe because we had it on our mind that first of all, this was also a way of converting money. We certainly did not intend to start spending money and buying things later when we had such opportunity to get the best things where we were. I had cocktail dresses, shoes, suits, coats, and a wonderful sheepskin coat (suede outside, fur inside). That's what I wore throughout the winter, I also had hats and boots.

Although you couldn't bring out personal belongings like a gold chain or other valuables, and I even had the suitcases made to order; linen suitcases, very light but huge, big to hold a lot of things. I did buy gloves in Paris, because they were known for their quality and work.

In Paris, we made arrangements for the crossing to New York. We learned that we could take a Swedish boat, the S.S. *Drottning-holm,* which would sail for America from the Swedish port of Göteborg. We found that this would give us time for a brief vacation on the Riviera before taking a train and ferry to Sweden. We did not know how soon we would be able to afford a vacation in France again, especially on the Riviera!

You can imagine that for someone like me, coming from times of deprivation and hardship, everything the Riviera had to offer was an absolute thrill. I remember that when we checked in at the Hotel Ruhl in Nice, and I flung open the window of our room and saw the Mediterranean in front of me, I was sure I was in heaven.

The trip from France to Sweden was long. In Copenhagen our train was put aboard a ferry to take us across the narrow part of the Baltic Sea that separated Denmark from Sweden there.

Göteborg was—and still is—a very beautiful seaport, with an old-fashioned sort of charm. We checked into a very old-fashioned hotel that had magnificent rooms and public lounges—but no private baths. If you wanted to take a bath, you had to go to a special bathroom. But there you really got the works. When Pista and I reported for our bath, two women attendants were waiting for us. The one led Pista to another section, while the other woman took charge of me. It was a whole ceremony; the attendant gave me a real beauty bath, complete with sponges, loofas and invigorating showers. Then I was pummeled dry and massaged. In the meantime, Pista was given the same service in the men's section. We both came out refreshed and ready to enjoy the city.

I think we only had two and a half days in Göteborg before our boat was ready to sail. I had never been on an ocean liner before. I had always loved the water but the only sailing experience I'd ever had was in rowboats, sailboats or small motorboats on Lake Balaton. And so the S.S. *Drottningholm* looked to me like a huge seagoing wonder, although I learned afterwards that she was by far not as big as the *Queen Mary* or the *Queen Elizabeth*.

The food aboard boat was lavish and exquisite. The tables in the dining hall were beautifully set, and there was a huge buffet, the *smorgasbord*, complete with delicacies I'd always loved: smoked fish, smoked meats, and delicious pastries.

The next morning I went out on deck, to a beautiful sight. The sea all around us was covered with ice; it looked as if our boat was in the midst of an ice-skating rink. In front of the boat, attached to it by strong cables, was an ice-breaker, with a heavy blade on its bow to cut the ice so that we could pass through. I lay down on one of the deck chairs and had my lunch served to me on deck —it was a wonderful experience.

On our second day out, the ice-breaker left us and we hit the open ocean. And then all hell broke loose. From one minute to the next it was as if we were on a roller coaster. Within minutes, everybody who'd been out on deck with me disappeared inside. I was left on deck all by myself. Something told me that as long as I stayed out in the fresh air I would not get seasick. Besides, I told myself that it was all in my mind, and as long as I took it into my head that I would not get sick, nothing would happen. Those who fled to the cabins were not so fortunate. The cabins were luxurious but they were very small, tiny cells, very much closed in—the best way to get really seasick. I was determined to stay outdoors as long as possible, going to our cabin only for the night. I even insisted on having all my meals served to me on deck. I lounged in the deck chair, or took brisk walks around the deck, and had a wonderful time. And in all our ten days at sea, I never, never got seasick, not even once. Pista was not so fortunate.

The SS *Drottningholm* sailed into New York harbor on February 23, 1947, at about six o'clock in the morning. I had been awake most of the night because we were told that we would pass the Statue of Liberty and we were eager to see it. By five o'clock I was out on deck. Gradually, the other passengers came out, too, but most of them didn't look so good, and some of the young men had sprouted beards because, at least for nine days, they'd been too seasick to shave!

My first sight of the Statue of Liberty is something I will never forget. To me it was the greatest symbol of freedom, as it was— and will be—for millions of others. I was close to tears because I had always dreamed about America, and now, at last, we were there.

A couple of hours later our boat docked. I remember that it had been snowing in New York and the snow was very high. We were luckier than most other refugees, because we had relatives waiting for us at the pier: Charlie Zucker's wife, Lottie, and

Nathan Zucker's wife, Pauline. They had never met us before, but there they were, welcoming us with open arms.

We had cabled the Zuckers to make reservations for us at a hotel. They told us they'd made the reservations but insisted that we go to the hotel only if we didn't like the room Nathan and Pauline had prepared for us at their own apartment on West 86th Street. I remember how Nathan's three children—they were still very young then—took me by the hand and led me to their own room, which their parents had fixed up for Pista and me. Everything had been arranged to make us as comfortable as possible, down to the last powder puff for me and a red rose in a bud vase.

It was difficult to refuse Nathan's and Pauline's hospitality, but we wanted to be on our own and checked into the hotel nearby. At that time Rickele, Nathan's and Charlie's mother, was still alive. Every Saturday afternoon the old lady's sons, daughters-in-law and grandchildren gathered at her apartment for Sabbath tea. Rickele, who was my mother's first cousin by marriage, took us to her heart immediately. She had made sure that her children and grandchildren knew all about their uncle Henrick Zucker, my grandfather, who'd done so many marvelous things for the family during World War I. I think it was mainly thanks to her stories that all the Zuckers in New York gave such a warm reception to Pista and me, and later to my parents, and to my cousin Zoltan when he arrived in America.

I wrote to my mother in Budapest every day. She saved some of my letters and cables in a scrapbook, together with pictures we sent her from New York, and she brought it with her when she came to the United States. So we have a fairly complete record of our early days in the United States.

The first thing we did was ask the Zuckers for the name of a good immigration lawyer who would be able to help us extend our American tourist visas. Nathan referred us to such a man; his name was Joe Abrams. When we saw Mr. Abrams at his office he told us that he could probably get a brief extension of our transit visas but he could not do so indefinitely. We would have to make definite arrangements for going on to Australia.

But I had no desire to go to Australia. I wanted to settle in the

United States. To me, America was paradise; the family was here, and so were the opportunities. It was everything I had ever wanted. And since New York represented America to me, as it did to most other newcomers from Europe, I wanted to remain in New York City.

On our second visit to his office, Mr. Abrams said to me, with a shy smile, that one way in which we could settle permanently in the United States would be if I got pregnant and had a baby born in this country. The baby would then be an American citizen by birth, and we'd be allowed to stay in order to raise him here.

Once again, luck was on our side. I had reason to think that I was indeed pregnant! Pauline Zucker took me to Dr. Berson, the family obstetrician, who had good news for me. I was going to have a baby! Now I was determined that my baby would not be a refugee in some temporary haven but a real Yankee. Joe Abrams went to work in earnest, and our transit visas were extended over and over again.

We didn't want to stay at the hotel any longer. We took an old-fashioned, very large apartment, the kind that's typical of New York's West Side. It was on West Seventy-second Street, between Broadway and Amsterdam Avenue, not far from where the Zuckers lived. A great many Jews from Austria and Hungary were then living in the neighborhood.

Also, Pista went into business. Because, officially, he was only a transient in the United States, he could not accept a job or set up a business under his own name, but he found a way to establish himself. He became a partner in a textile factory in Paterson, New Jersey, whose owner was a widow. Her husband, the original owner, had just died and she did not want to run the business by herself. So, according to the partnership agreement, the business would continue under her name, but Pista would do certain work and would be entitled to a share of the earnings.

However, my husband felt restless and unsettled. No matter how nice it was in New York, and no matter what his chances in Paterson, he suddenly announced that we should not give up the idea of going to Australia. Australia, he insisted, was the land of the future. Our Australian immigration visas were still valid; if we allowed them to expire without using them, we might never be able to go there and we might be sorry for the rest of our lives that we missed the opportunity. That's what Pista said, and he wouldn't listen to any counterarguments from me.

The only obstacle that kept Pista from packing our bags then and there was the fact that for the first few weeks of my pregnancy I was throwing up every day and couldn't travel even by subway from one part of New York to the other. How, then, could I have made the journey, partly by transcontinental train and partly by air, from New York halfway across the world to Australia? Nevertheless, Pista insisted that we make preparations to go. He even made me send one set of baby clothes straight to our friends the Safranys in Sydney, to await our arrival.

In order to raise cash, we gathered all the silver we had sent piecemeal to New York from Budapest and put it on display at our apartment. One by one, the Zuckers and their friends came, including the ladies from Pauline's Hadassah chapter, and bought the silver articles. The things were beautiful and practically sold themselves. Silver was a good investment, and also good for display in your living room showcase. I was selling the silver like hotcakes.

Because of my terrible "morning sickness," the only chance I had to eat a decent meal was in the evening. My favorite food was chicken bones, which I still like. For a fast pick-me-up, I loved to go to the Horn and Hardart automat. In those days there was such a place on almost every corner. You threw in a nickel and out came a glass of milk or buttermilk, which helped keep me in fairly good shape.

During the fifth month of my pregnancy, my vomiting stopped. I was able to get around a little more. I even performed a few "good deeds," welcoming friends and relatives from Hungary who were beginning to arrive in New York. One of those who came was my father's niece, Anci Lowy, cousin of Irene Szecsi (the cousin who was reunited with her husband at my parents' apartment in Budapest). I not only met Anci at the pier when her boat arrived but took her into our apartment on West Seventy-second Street to stay with us.

Anci did not speak a word of English, and Pista's knowledge of English wasn't much better. So I made both of them take English lessons. Pauline Zucker took Anci under her wing and when Anci was able to speak English after a fashion, Pauline arranged speaking engagements for her at various Hadassah chapters. Pista would correct the rough drafts of Anci's speeches, all of which dealt with her experiences in the concentration camps. Eventually Anci married a man whom she met through a friend of Pauline's. So she had a husband and family of her own and no longer needed help from me.

Meanwhile, Pista went ahead with arrangements for our journey to Australia. We left New York in August 1947, six months after we'd landed there. When we boarded the transcontinental train for San Francisco at Grand Central Station, forty-seven members—near and remote—of the Zucker family were there to say good-bye.

Pista and I spent three days and three nights on the train to San Francisco. It was not a very pleasant journey for me, because I was convinced that we were not doing the right thing, while Pista felt that his decision had been the only right one. I realized then that, for the first time, my husband and I were in complete disagreement on a very important question.

I remember that we had one rest stop—in Chicago. We got out and I felt as if I'd walked into a boiler. The temperature was 100 degrees, and God knows how much humidity. I felt as if I had suddenly caught fire.

San Francisco, on the other hand, was—and still is—a beautiful city. I was absolutely enchanted. We had a few days there and were able to use the time to tour all the interesting places because the climate in San Francisco was much better than in the East. You generally don't need air conditioning in San Francisco, not even at the height of summer.

But then our stay in San Francisco came to an end. And there we were, at the airport, waiting for the Clipper (that's what they called the overseas planes then) that would take us across the Pacific to Australia. I was not unhappy; once I make up my mind, I leave every thought behind, and concentrate on the future. I was young; my life was ahead of me. Although I had thoughts of regret, and you can't live with regret—you have to go ahead. We were looking ahead, and I saw that, even in my husband's behavior or attitude, he felt he was making a mistake but he just had to do it now or otherwise he wouldn't have peace of mind.

While I was standing at the airport in San Francisco, as far as I remember, even as I was only having thoughts about what lay ahead, in America, I had found everything that I anticipated, everything that I wanted, everything that I thought would be here, and now I was leaving it behind. There was nothing to think about anymore. If you were to ask me what my thoughts were during the months I was in the United States, that's another story.

I don't remember going through a period of adjustment because you adjust to things that are good much faster than to things that are bad. And you just walk into them and you enjoy goodness for what it is, as I remember I did. I enjoyed walking on Times Square, under all kinds of circumstances. I enjoyed the qualities of the people and the quantities and the abundance of everything. When I first saw Lindy's window there was a huge cheesecake, beside gigantic apples and mammoth strawberries. I will never forget it. I mean, I thought this was the greatest thing that ever happened and here it was at my fingertips. Who could ask for anything more and people who were so kind and helpful?

Compared to Budapest, of course, here it was all bigger and greater even just its size. But the automobiles were—well, that's not my cup of tea. The skyscrapers, yes, and I remember when Pauline first took me by my hand to Radio City Music Hall and she sat down and she was holding my hand like a little child or a lover, I was oohing and aahing and I refused to believe such a thing could really be—all those Rockettes moving at the same time as if pulled on strings and that tremendous show, which also changed every month. So, from then on I never missed a single month—every month when the program changed, we went to Radio City Music Hall. It was a tremendous bargain. I think it was $1.75 or something and you could sit there for four hours—see a floor show, listen to beautiful music, some marvelous dancers, and see a movie too and be in such fantastic surroundings. I made it my business after that that whoever—friend, relative or acquaintance—came to New York, that was the first trip. I took them to Radio City Music Hall because I thought that really represented something very American, and it is.

Other memories were with me, for instance, I was very much impressed that I could go into a store and buy a brassiere in my size, to my measurements, and then walk out with it without having to have it made-to-order as I used to do all the time. And, when I found out they had even mail-order catalogues that allow you to order from the remotest places of the United States—for instance, brassieres by mail-order—that really floored me. I was tremendously impressed with it. The same thing with bathing suits. I arrived with quite a selection of bikinis made for me by the same lingerie shop. The lingerie makers of Budapest were very famous for all kinds of underwear and I must say that my bikinis were a sensation everywhere I went. They were so modern and well made that on the American beaches, not only were they not known yet but some of the places didn't even allow women to wear them. So talking about clothes, then of course, when I went into certain stores and found out that for very little money, very little, you could buy very nice well-fitted clothes, in addition to very expensive things. Everybody had a way of dressing and everybody was well dressed because the clothes were affordable to people in all walks of life. The only thing I could never understand was how a lady could go shopping at ten o'-clock in the morning with a feathered hat and with a fur coat and all kinds of other (to me) very dressy items, an outfit I would only wear in the evening. I mean, I saw that some people didn't have discrimination. They had the clothes so they just wore them. The same way I could never understand why somebody could show up at a funeral in a red hat or red dress or something that was out of place. But I guess that I was amazed because I grew up with different customs and traditions. Now, when I left the United States, of course, I had to buy maternity clothes and I got myself outfitted with two or three very pretty looking dresses, also already made which of course I had never experienced there. But they looked good and fitted nicely and were chic and little did

I know that when I arrived in Australia, there I would really create a sensation because they were back—I don't know how many years—when I arrived in my American ready-made maternity clothes. Everybody copied my wardrobe—they thought that it was the greatest thing they'd ever seen.

The flight from San Francisco to Sydney, Australia, was the first time I had ever been up in an airplane. The plane we were assigned to board had some problems, so after some waiting, it was announced we would be the first passengers on a Pan American Clipper that was equipped with berths with curtains, like the old-fashioned sleeping cars on railroad trains. This was a sensational way to travel in comfort. Of course, this was much before the fast jets and the trip took three days and three nights.

Our first fuel stop was Canton Island, one of a group of coral islands in the Pacific. The only noteworthy feature of this island, which is controlled by the United States, was a kind of hangar used by Pan-American Airways for refueling. We were told that we would be there for only an hour or so. We got off the plane and looked around. Canton Island was a miserable place, full of mosquitoes and other nasty, little insects. It was also terribly hot and humid. We were escorted into the hangar and told to make ourselves comfortable. The personnel passed around little hors d' oeuvres that looked very appetizing. I thought they were spread with chicken liver pate, until I bit into one and almost got sick. The taste was so different from chicken liver that I thought maybe the pate had spoiled in the heat. When I complained that something seemed to be wrong with the chicken liver, I was told that it wasn't chicken liver at all but peanut butter! That was my first encounter with peanut butter, and ever since then, the very thought of peanut butter is enough to make me sick.

After about 45 minutes, the pilot announced that the plane was ready for takeoff. I felt I didn't care if I never saw Canton Island again, and I said so. But only a few minutes after takeoff the pilot announced that some kind of trouble had developed with one of the propellers and we would have to return to Canton Island! Since then, I've always said, "Never say, 'Never,' because you never know what the future will bring." We had to stay on Canton Island half that night.

Our next stop was a little more interesting: Samoa, capital of the Fiji Islands. When our plane landed, a band of natives came out to serenade us. They were beautiful people with bushy hair and grass skirts; their chests were covered with ribbons and medals. They even gave us a little tour of the town while our plane took on new fuel.

Later, one of the stewards on our plane told us an amusing story of how primitive and superstitious these natives really were. There were big fruit plantations on Samoa, where large numbers of native laborers were employed. Well, it seems that one day the owner of one of these plantations came out to the field where all the natives were working. He took off the glasses he was wearing, placed them carefully on a fence and said, "I'll be back at six o'clock this evening. Meanwhile, I'm leaving my glasses here. They will be watching over you while I am away. So continue your work just as you would if I were here." According to our steward, the natives really believed that these eyeglasses were part of their boss and able to take his place while he was away. And so they worked diligently all day long. Otherwise, the steward said, they'd probably have sat on the ground all day, sunning themselves.

Our last stop before Sydney was Honolulu, where we spent a few beautiful days. In those days Honolulu was not as commercialized as it is today, and everything was still in its original, native beauty.

When we arrived in Sydney, the Safranys were at the airport. Of course it wasn't the same as family but they were very nice and tried their best to make us comfortable. Nevertheless, Sydney certainly was not anything like New York.

Being a visitor in Sydney at that time was fine—from Monday to Saturday. But on Sunday, Sydney was the most frustrating place. They had blue laws which were strictly enforced. So there was no place to go for dinner or for a drink on Sunday, and unless you had friends who invited you, Sunday was a day of unrelieved boredom.

I met other friends from Hungary who'd gone to Australia. In the beginning, they'd written us enthusiastic letters claiming that Australia was paradise. But now it was clear that they had not found their paradise in Sydney, yet and they had become bitter and frustrated. Eventually, most of them did well in Australia, but in those days things definitely did not look promising. And as far as I was concerned, Sydney certainly was not anything even remotely like New York.

Before long, Pista, too, realized that Australia was not the place for him. I remember that he and I took long walks on the waterfront, up and down, up and down. All around us there were sailors on shore leave, looking for a good time. But Pista was in a state of utter gloom, wondering how we could get back to the United States. This was not an easy task, but my husband always knew how to talk to administrators and authorities, and he started to work on possibilities to return to America as legitimate immigrants.

In the meantime, since we had nothing better to do while waiting for a decision from the American consulate, we looked around a little in Sydney and its surroundings. It was August, and the height of winter. The weather was damp and chilly, and the heating completely inadequate. All the houses had stone floors—tile and stone—which didn't help to warm you up.

Somebody suggested that we leave Sydney for a weekend and go to a beautiful resort hotel in the Blue Mountains nearby that had just opened. Pista and I took the advice and took off for the Blue Mountains.

The hotel looked modern and attractive. Unlike many other places we'd seen during our few weeks in Australia, this one even had central heating. But at night, when we turned on the radiator in our room, no heat came. Later, we found out that instead of going into the rooms, all the heat from the central heating system was going outdoors. For some reason the pipes of the radiators had been arranged in such a way that they could heat only the air outside, not the air in the rooms!

At five o'clock the next morning there was a knock on our door. It was breakfast: tea, bread and butter. This, apparently, was the hotel's idea of an English-style breakfast—tea, with about a dozen little bread triangles sliced paper-thin!

So much for the wonderful resort hotel in the Blue Mountains.

Early in September, Pista found a way for us to return to the United States. He explained to the American consul in Sydney that we were disappointed in Australia and had no other choice but to go back where we had come from. He was afraid that it would have to be Hungary. But the only way in which you could go from Australia to Hungary then was by way of the American continent. So voilà, once again we received American transit visas, entitling us to pass through the United States, this time, supposedly, on our way to Hungary!

Once again we left Sydney by air. Three days later we landed on American soil—not in San Francisco this time but in Los Angeles. Altogether, we had been away from the United States for only a little over six weeks. It was now mid-September and I was in the seventh month of my pregnancy. Of course there was the law under which a female alien visiting the United States was eligible for a permanent immigration visa if she gave birth to a child in this country. However, for this very reason, the American authorities had a sharp eye out for foreign female visitors in an advanced stage of pregnancy. I did not want any trouble, so when we entered U.S. customs at the Los Angeles airport, I wrapped myself into a wide, loose coat to hide my figure.

In New York, the whole family was waiting for us at the station. We'd been away less than two months, but during that time we'd journeyed halfway around the world.

Pista and I had to start again from scratch in New York. We had given up our apartment on West Seventy-second Street. So we had to rent a hotel room while we looked for an apartment. We heard that a nice modern building was going up in our old neighborhood, on West Seventy-sixth Street, between Riverside Drive and West End Avenue. So we went to the rental agent and registered for an apartment in the building, which we were told would be ready for occupancy very shortly. I mentioned to the agent that I was expecting a child in two months' time, in November, and the agent assured me that our apartment would be ready long before that. So we signed the lease on the apartment and looked forward happily to moving into this new apartment with our child. We were real "greenhorns"; we didn't know as yet how builders and contractors operate in the United States.

Meanwhile, Pista was looking around for business opportunities. He wanted to remain in textile manufacturing, working with upholstery fabrics. He sought out business acquaintances he'd made in New York before we went to Australia. We learned that Adrian Heller, who'd visited us in Budapest and had given us the ten-dollar bill from our unknown friend in America, was back in New York, also his good friend Béla Kármán. Pista contacted them and although they knew nothing about textiles, they were sufficiently impressed with Pista's ideas to make him a business proposition. They were willing to invest some money in a partnership with him. So Pista got the capital he needed for his textile factory. He took a place in Paterson, New Jersey and started buying Jacquard looms and other equipment.

While Pista and his partners were engaged in setting up the factory, I was busy getting together the things we would need for our new apartment. We had expected the building to be ready for occupancy in a matter of weeks. But here I was, in my ninth month, and the apartment wasn't ready yet. What if I had the baby before our apartment was ready? The hotel management informed us that they didn't permit babies in the hotel. Where could we go with the baby then? And so we lived from day to day, hoping for a miracle to happen.

The miracle came to pass in the form of my wonderful obstetrician, Dr. Berson. He told me he would make inquiries at two of the hospitals where he practiced, to see whether they would be willing to keep my baby after my discharge, if necessary. Whichever of the two hospitals would agree to keep my baby would be the one to which he would take me for the delivery. He called me the very next day with a "yes" answer from Sydenham Hospital, which was in the middle of Harlem. I accepted Dr. Berson's suggestion because I trusted him implicitly.

The first signs that the baby might be on the way came on a Friday night, just as we finished dinner at the apartment of Nathan and Pauline Zucker. I had no pains, but we called Dr. Berson. He suggested that as long as I had no pains I should go out and take a little walk. Then, if I felt no better, or the pains should begin, I should telephone him again and check into Sydenham.

Nathan, himself the father of three, said, "Okay, Marianne, let's go take a walk!" So Nathan, Pauline, Pista, and I left the house and walked up and down Broadway, up and down. Finally, at eleven o'clock, Nathan and Pauline walked us back to our hotel, which was on West Ninety-first Street, only a few blocks away from their apartment building.

Before going to bed, I reported again to Dr. Berson, who suggested that I go to sleep and call him again the next morning. The next morning there was still nothing new, but when I phoned Dr. Berson, he told me to go to the hospital.

That morning it was raining cats and dogs—a deluge. It was impossible to get a cab. While Pista sloshed back and forth on the flooded street, vainly hailing every cab that passed, I sat waiting in the hotel lobby, becoming more and more anxious by the minute. At one point, I think, I lost consciousness. The next thing I felt was someone holding my arm and guiding me into a car. A nice gentleman had realized our plight and volunteered to drive Pista and me in his own car to the hospital, which, actually, was not too far away, on West 125th Street.

Late that afternoon, at last, I went into labor. My son was born exactly ten minutes before midnight, on November 8, 1947. I named him Ronald, a name I considered thoroughly American, with no Hungarian equivalent. I wanted my son to be American through and through, from the very start of his life.

The next morning my husband's partners came to visit me and asked me to suggest a name for our new factory. We thought it would be appropriate to have the newly-established factory bear the name of the part owner's new-born son, and so I proposed the name "Ronnietex Jacquard Mills." My suggestion was promptly accepted by both Pista and his partners.

Eight days later we celebrated Ronnie's *b'rith*. I thought about what I'd been hearing from Hungary: even now that the war was over, Jewish mothers in Hungary were afraid to have their baby sons circumcised. In America, even then, almost 40 years ago, many gentile boys were also circumcised, but in Hungary circumcision was a sure sign that the boy was Jewish. And so many Hungarians who had survived the Holocaust feared that circumcising their baby sons was in fact marking them for death if anti-Semitism ever got the upper hand again. My own sister-in-law, Klári Vayda, had a son after the war and did not have him circumcised. Eventually, many such boys underwent circumcision by their own choice when they grew up. Some chose to do this when they were already in their thirties, when it's a painful operation, but they wanted to have it done because they were proud to be Jewish and wanted to bear the physical mark of Jewish identity. As far as I was concerned, it never occurred to me even for a moment not to have Ronnie circumcised. I was proud to be Jewish and to let the world know that I had given birth to a Jewish boy.

As soon as my mother in Budapest learned that I was pregnant she wrote to me that, come hell or high water, she would come to New York to be with me when I gave birth to my baby. But there were some complications. First of all, there was our visit to Australia. Also, Hungarian exit permits and American visas didn't always go together. Nevertheless, at the last minute, Mother managed to obtain a passport, complete with Hungarian exit permit and a visitor's visa to the United States. Leave it to a veteran travel agent!

She packed one suitcase, left my father and the apartment on Akacfá 6, and just took off. She had broken her leg a few weeks earlier and her cast had just been removed, but such little things could never stop Aranka Lowy!

Her first stop was London, and there she had to break her trip because of the thick fog. In those days before stratospheric jets, planes couldn't take off in foggy weather. So she had to spend several days in London, waiting for the fog to lift and for space on a plane bound for New York.

Mother arrived in New York ten days after Ronnie was born. And I think I should add here that luck was with us once again:

despite our fears, and although the apartment on West Seventy-sixth Street was not ready, waiting to receive the new baby and the new grandmother, the hospital did keep Ronnie the few weeks until we could finally settle once and forever, into our new life in America!

ARANKA

After my daughter Marianne and her husband Pista, I was the first of the "Hungarian Zuckers" to land on the American continent. Two years later, my nephew Zoltan Weiss arrived in New York and his sister Eva (with her second husband and their little son) settled in Canada. My father and his wife stayed in Budapest and died there. America might be rich with fruit, Father said to me before I left, but to get at the fruit you still had to shake the trees, and he didn't think he was strong enough anymore to shake the trees. . . . But he was always the happiest to know that Ronnie, his first great-grandchild, was born in the United States. In his letters, he called him "Prince Yitzhak" (Yitzhak is Ronnie's Hebrew name) and he thought it was a great thing that my daughter had started a new generation in America.

I was separated from my husband, Endre, for two and a half years. Once I was in the United States, I was able to get permanent immigration papers for myself, but I couldn't do the same for Endre. He had to spend 11 months in Cuba before the Americas let him in.

Meanwhile, in New York, I wanted to start a travel business. I spoke English and visited a few travel agencies. At the first agency to which I went they asked me, "How do you expect to do business in this country, when you don't really know anybody?" I told them that I had a very large family here, who knew a lot of people. I'd send out circulars and we'd be in business. So the man said, "All right, try it. I'm willing to work with you." When I came back to this agency the next time, the boss said, "I had no idea you really had such a large family. I just got a phone call from a Mr. Charles Zucker. He said he was your cousin and ordered tickets to Australia. Six tickets, no less!"

I worked with that agency for many years. As a travel agent, I was able to help many Hungarian Jews leave Hungary and come to the United States. First, I would arrange for them to purchase visas for Cuba. This I did with the help of a Jewish man who had connections in Havana, with the Cuban government. With those Cuban visas in their hands, the refugees could get American transit visas so they could pass through the United States on the way to Cuba. Of course, these people never went to Cuba. They found ways of staying in the United States, often with my help. The State Department didn't like what I was doing, working with the Cuban government; they thought it was like being a foreign agent. They also didn't like it that I was helping to bring so many immigrants into the United States. So at one point the State Department sent me a letter saying I was *persona non grata.* They could have deported me to Hungary. But I didn't care what the State Department thought. I acted as if I never heard that I was *persona non grata.* And then there was the change in the Cuban government; Cuba went Communist and everything was different. So nobody bothered me about being *persona non grata* anymore.

My husband, Endre, arrived in New York from Cuba in 1949. In addition to my travel work, I was then doing IKKA business. This meant I arranged for people in New York to send money to their relatives in Hungary. When Endre came, I turned the IKKA work over to him. Of course he also helped me in the travel business. He was a very kind man and made friends easily. And whenever he met people, he'd give them our business card immediately. In this way, my husband got me some very good business.

Endre and I had ten years together in New York. Then he went on a visit to Budapest. He wanted to set up travel and hotel arrangements to make it easier for Americans to visit relatives in

Hungary. From Budapest, he planned to go to Rome. There, he was going to meet me and we would go together on a trip to Israel before returning to New York. Goodhearted as he was, Endre always thought of others before thinking about himself. When he left New York for Budapest, he was carrying dozens of packages and messages from people in New York to relatives and friends in Hungary. From Budapest, he made a side trip to his old home town, Büdszentmihaly, to visit the graves of his parents. He returned to Budapest with a terrible cold. All the same, he made arrangements to go on to Vienna as planned so he could meet me in Rome.

But then Lujza, our former maid, visited him at his hotel in Budapest. She saw that my husband was in a terrible shape. So she said to him, "Stay here in Budapest, Mr. Lowy. You can't travel in this condition. You are sick." But Endre wouldn't listen and left Budapest for Vienna. In Vienna he got worse. He had more than just a cold; there was a kidney infection. Anyway, one day I received a cable from Hungarian friends in Vienna that I should come at once because Endre was seriously ill. Marianne and I took the next plane to Vienna.

Three days after we arrived there, my husband passed away. He died on July 13, 1959. It was a terrible day in my life.

Of one thing I was sure: we wanted my husband's grave to be in the United States, not in Vienna and certainly not in Hungary. I applied to Pan American Airlines for permission to have Endre's body shipped back to the United States aboard the same plane on which Marianne and I would return to New York.

And so my daughter and I brought Endre back to New York and buried him in Woodridge, New Jersey, in an Orthodox Jewish cemetery where many of our very religious friends from Hungary are buried.

Afterwards, I did what Endre would have wanted me to do. I continued with my life. I am almost eighty years old now, and no longer able to get around easily, but I still carry on my travel business from my apartment, on the West Side of New York. I believe that God gave me long life so I could enjoy my own life and see my daughter happy.

Marianne's life in the United States at first was not easy. Her husband, Pista, died in 1969. At that time her son, Ronnie, was away at medical school in Brussels. Her daughter, Vivian, was just seventeen years old. Pista left very little money, so Marianne had to support herself and help pay for her children's education by giving physical culture classes. Thank God, she was able to make a living for herself and put her children through school: Ronnie is a gynecologist in New York, and Vivian attended the Museum School in Boston, one of the best art schools in the United States.

In 1974, Marianne remarried and moved to Columbus, Ohio, with her husband, Benjamin Balshone. He is a pharmacist, a very fine man and a good son-in-law. Both of them visit me in New York very often, and of course we call each other on the phone all the time.

Marianne has four grandchildren now, so I am a great-grandmother. This is a very big thing; not many Jewish women my age who were in Hungary during the war have survived to see their great-grandchildren. Many of them have no great-grandchildren at all because their families were wiped out by the Germans.

Marianne's son Ronnie, in New York, has two children, a boy of two, and a little girl who was just born. Their mother, who is from the Philippines, is not Jewish, but we had a *b'rith* for the boy, who is named Steven after his grandfather. (Pista's real name was Istvan, the Hungarian for Steven; Pista is a pet name for Istvan.) I hope I will live to see both these children come closer to Judaism.

Marianne's daughter Vivian is married in Toronto to a nice young man of Polish descent by the name of Irving Garten. Irving was born in Canada, but his parents survived the Holocaust, his father, in Siberia. They came to Canada from Poland after the war. Vivian is an artist. Irvin has a very interesting, unusual occupation; he rebuilds old houses. They have two children, a boy and a girl, just like Ronnie and his wife, except that with Vivian, it is the girl, Ariel, who came before the boy. Ariel is now four years old; her little brother, Joel, is two. Ariel's middle name is Stephanie, in memory of her grandfather. Joel's Hebrew name is Elíyahu, after my husband.

As far as I am concerned, I am content. I have everything I want. I thank G-d for my family, and for the energy he gave me to carry on my work. I want to be active until my last moment. G-d should only give me good health.

Europe's Pustule of Social Disease

New York Times.

NEW YORK, MONDAY, JUNE 29, 1914.—EIGHTEEN PAGES.

ONE CENT In Greater New York, Jersey City and Newark. TWO CENTS

Becoming northwest.
[For full weather report see Page 17.]

HEIR TO AUSTRIA'S THRONE IS SLAIN WITH HIS WIFE BY A BOSNIAN YOUTH TO AVENGE SEIZURE OF HIS COUNTRY

Francis Ferdinand Shot During State Visit to Sarajevo.

TWO ATTACKS IN A DAY

...uke Saves His Life First by Knocking Aside a ...b Hurled at Auto.

SECOND ATTEMPT

...s at Car as the Royal ...turn from Town Hall Kills Both of Them.

...O A SERVIAN PLOT

...and Not to Go to Bosnia. Populace Met ...ian Flags.

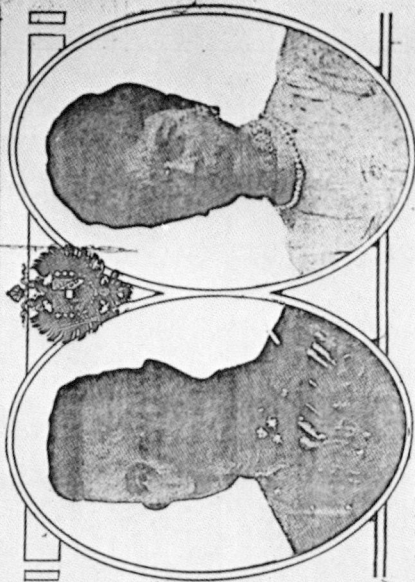

Archduke Francis Ferdinand and his Consort the Duchess of Hohenberg

Slain by Assassin's Bullets.

BOURSES OF EUROPE

London Market Inactive, but...
Steady—Prices Firm in
Paris, Higher in Berlin.

Styles of Dresses Designed for the Fall Trade.

The Pustule ruptures spilling its poison indiscriminately

Ego prevents cure

FIGHT

BELA KUN OUSTED; MODERATES TAKE HUNGARIAN RULE

Red Chief's Fall Forced by Allies' Warning and Crushing Defeat of His Army.

BELA KUN OUSTED; ARMY BROKEN IN RIOTS REBU

VOL. LXVIII...NO.

Lander and Boehm, Chief Lately In Jail Communist Govern

Reported Streaming Back the Czech Front

HENRY FORD STILL THINKS SOLDIERS ARE MURDERERS

BELA KUN A PRISONER.

SSITYWHOLLYLACKING

PEIDLL BECOMES PREMIER

TROOPS STRAGGLE

Utter Demoralization Ha

Capt. Gregory, American Food Official, Credited

ANTI-RED ARMY GROW

Now Said to Number More

125,000 Man—Peasants K

Food from

OUST BELA KUN, ALLIES DEMAND

FORD SAYS PRESS AND THE BANKERS GOT US INTO WAR

Hungarians Told by Clemenceau They Cannot Get Food or Supplies Till They Do.

PARIS, July 31.—A strong, arraign-

Deposed Head of Magyar Sovi Kept Isolated, Vienna Hears

COPENHAGEN, July 31.—Bela Hungarian

ALLIED ULTIMA TO MAGYAR REDS?

Reported Threat to Oc

Budapest Unless Bela Ku

Government Unless Resign

Warns on Austrian Ships Mutiny.

Czechs

KUN PROPOSES CONFERENCE

Wants All States of Former Austrian Empire to Get Together.

Copyright, 1919, by The Chicago Tribune Co.
Bela Kun, June 24. (via Paris, July 1.)

TERROR TROOPS SEIZE BUDAPEST

FRIEDRICH HOLDS ON TO POWER IN HUNGARY

Socialists Refuse to Join Premier and Attempt to Form New Cabinet Fails.

VIENNA, Aug. 27.—According to in-

ASKS HUNGARY FOR KUN.

Hungary Also Seeks Extradition of Red Leader's Associates.

BASEL, Aug. 27.

SILENT ON BARRING MAURER

State Department Gives No Reason for Recalling Passport.

1919

Blame someone

A quack uses the blamed to conceal his legerdemain

The New York Times.

"All the News That's Fit to Print."

VOL. LXXXVIII... No. 29,805.

Entered as Second-Class Matter, Postoffice, New York, N. Y.

Copyright, 1939, by The New York Times Company.

NEW YORK, FRIDAY, SEPTEMBER 1, 1939.

EXTRA

Partly cloudy and somewhat warmer today. Tomorrow generally fair with moderate temperatures.

Temperatures Yesterday—Max., 67; Min., 61

THREE CENTS NEW YORK CITY | FOUR CENTS Elsewhere Except and Vicinity | in 7th and 8th Postal Zones

GERMAN ARMY ATTACKS POLAND; CITIES BOMBED, PORT BLOCKADED; DANZIG IS ACCEPTED INTO REICH

Hitler Gives Wor

In a Proclamation H Accuses Warsaw of Appeal to Arms

FOREIGNERS ARE WARN

They Remain in Poland at O: Risk—Nazis to Shoot at At Planes Flying Over Reich

By OTTO D. TOLISCHUS
Special Cable to THE NEW YORK TIMES
BERLIN, Friday, Sept. 1 Charging that Germany had b attacked, Chancellor Hitler at

Hitler Acts Against Poland

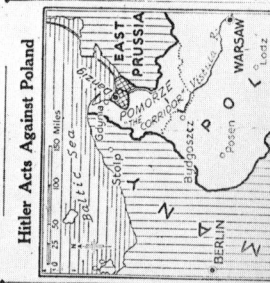

HOSTILITIES BEGUN

Warsaw Reports German Offensive Moving on Three Objectives

ROOSEVELT WARNS NAVY

Also Notifies Army Leaders of Warfare—Envoys Tell of Bombing of 4 Cities

By JERRY SZAPIRO
Special Cable to THE NEW YORK TIMES
DANZIG, Friday, Sept. 1.—

FREE CITY IS SEIZED

Forster Notifies Hitler of Order Putting Danzig Into the Reich

NAVY ACCEPTED BY CHANCELLOR

Poles Ready, Made Their Preparations After Hostilities Appeared Inevitable

Wireless to THE NEW YORK TIMES
DANZIG, Friday, Sept. 1.—

tins on Europe's Conflict

Reuters British news Polish sources in Paris that

Attack on Entire Front Reported
LONDON, Friday, Sept. 1 (AP).—A Reuters dispatch from Paris said

PARIS SAYS CORSETS

But What Will the American Woman Say?

Nothing can save the patient

CROATS RALLY TO SERBS' SIDE;
HUNGARY'S PREMIER SUICIDE;
BRITISH EVACUATE BENGAZI

YUGOSLAVS UNITED

Matchek Takes Cabinet
Post—Rome Recalls
Its Legation Staff

The International S---

FRIDAY, A---
The United States Government formally informed the Italian Embassy in Washington yesterday that Admiral Alberto Lais, the Italian naval attache, was persona non grata and requested his followers to ... upon ... every way the military ... preparations of the Yugoslav armed forces to resist a German invasion. The government declared Belgrade, Zagreb and Ljubljana open cities. (Page 1. Col-

Count Paul Teleki

By C. L. SULZBERGER

European, 1940

Count Teleki left farewell notes to his invalid wife and to the Hungarian Regent, Admiral Nicholas Horthy. There were reports that in the latter note he detailed his feeling that Hungary could no longer hold out against German domination and that his two-year efforts had failed. [The Swiss Telegraphic Agency said the note explained that "he no longer felt himself capable of fulfilling, his difficult and unhappy task."]

He is reported to have told the Cabinet last night:

"The future is hopeless."

The Foreign Office at first said the 62-year-old statesman died of a heart attack, but friends said he had taken poison, and subsequent reports said he shot himself in the head.

Only now can it be disclosed that Count Teleki was one of those behind the book, "Why Germany Cannot Win the War," which broke all sales records in Hungary. Count Teleki told the author, Ivan Lajos, that he intended to ban the book after it had sold 100,000 copies. He added that he would ban it before that unless a copy was put in the hands of every Hungarian Army officer.

An ocean of blood—we wring our hands

New York Times.

LATE CITY EDITION
Mostly cloudy with diminishing winds.
Temperatures Yesterday—Max. 34; Min. 25
Sunrise, 6:06 A. M.; Sunset, 7:09 P. M.

THREE CENTS new york city

Copyright, 1944, by The New York Times Company.

NEW YORK, TUESDAY, MARCH 21, 1944.

GERMAN TROOPS OCCUPY HUNGARY; WIDE RESISTANCE IS REPORTED; RED ARMY TAKES 2 KEY CENTERS

NAZIS STAGE COUP

Hungarian Regent and Others Believed Held After Hitler Parley

PRODDED FOR FURTHER AID

Leaders Said to Have Refused More Help Against Russians — Warning to Others Seen

By GEORGE AXELSSON
By Cable to The New York Times.
STOCKHOLM, Sweden, March 20—German troops were reported tonight to have marched into Hungary in a move to prop Adolf Hitler's weakened southeastern flank and to forestall a break in the Axis. . . .

MARCH OF RUSSIANS ECHOES IN SOUTHEAST EUROPE

MARCH 20, 1944
With the Red Army pushing steadily westward Hungary (2) that was reported to be encountering resistance, especially at the Austro-Hungarian border. In Rumania plans for evacuating (1, detailed map Page 2), Germany took steps to consolidate her position in the satellite countries. She embarked on a military occupation of Bucharest (3) were reported being speeded.

CASSINO...

SLIP IN REINFORCEMENTS

Friend and Foe Interlocked In Crazy Quilt of Lines a... Furious Battle Ra...

By C. L. S...

This 'Louis-Lane' Mail
Win Praise of Soldiers

HULL WELCOMES
INTEREST IN POLICY

Finds Attention of Congress
and Public Gratifying—Plans
Radio Talk on Topic

Plea Made for Hungarian Jews
Menaced by Nazi Occupation

Dr. Israel Goldstein, Back From
Britain, Says There Is Not an
Hour to Lose in Carrying Out
Large-Scale Rescue Action

OLD NAZI DEVICES
TRAPPED HUNGARY

Chutists, Soldiers Hidden Be-
low Barge Decks and Sealed
in Trains Pounced on Ally

By GEORGE AXELSSON

THE NEW YORK TIMES, WEDNESDAY, MARCH 22, 1944.

Dr. Israel Goldstein

HUNGARY LIQUIDATES
JEWISH BUSINESSES

16,000 of 30,000 Confiscated
With Aid of Gestapo

THE NEW YORK TIMES, THURSDAY, MAY 4, 1944

CAROL SAYS RUMANIA   HULL STUDIES UPSET

Surprise party for the condemned

GERMANY EXTENDS GRIP ON SATELLITES

Text of the Statement by Roosevelt

ROOSEVELT WARNS GERMANS ON JEWS

MEANS REFUGEE BOARD

U.S. NAVY DL... CANADIANS

Too little

June 6, 1944—too late

10,000 Berlin Civilians Drowned When Elite Guard Flooded Subway

Bodies of Those Who Clamored for End of War Still Seen—Horthy Armistice Signaled Murder of Hungary's Jews

THE NEW YORK TIMES, FRIDAY, AUGUST 11, 1944

Coup Foils Horthy Peace Bid; Nazis Tighten Hungary Rule

HORTHY PLEDGES JEWS AID

MORGAN IN PARIS

Rabid quack infects his centurions

SWEDEN SEEKS DIPLOMAT

Asks Russia to Free Man Who Disappeared in 1945

STOCKHOLM, Sweden, Nov. 12 (Reuters)—Sweden has asked Russia to free a Swedish diplomat taken prisoner by the Russian Army when it moved into Budapest in 1945.

The diplomat, Raoul Wallenberg, a secretary at the Swedish legation, was doing relief work among displaced persons and other war victims in Hungary.

Russia informed Sweden at the time that the army had taken care of Mr. Wallenberg during the general confusion but that he had later gone away.

In Sweden the belief persisted that Mr. Wallenberg was held prisoner in Russia. Former Soviet political prisoners have said they had talked with him in Russian labor camps as recently as Monday. …

JAPANESE WITNESS HERE
on Loss of Indianapolis

HUNGARY DOOMS BAINISS

Death for Ex-Minister as Traitor

—Szalasi Conviction Heard

BUDAPEST, Hungary, Dec. 8 …

REMEMBER THE NUDISTS!

Camp for Service Women
Opened South of Manila

BRITISH TO WITHDRAW
FORCES IN INDO-CHINA

All over—where are the criminals? Are there survivors? The world notices a missing hero

After thirty-five years, life and fashions reflect change and normalcy. Marianne arrives in New York. Those left behind have their memories. Has the disease been eradicated?

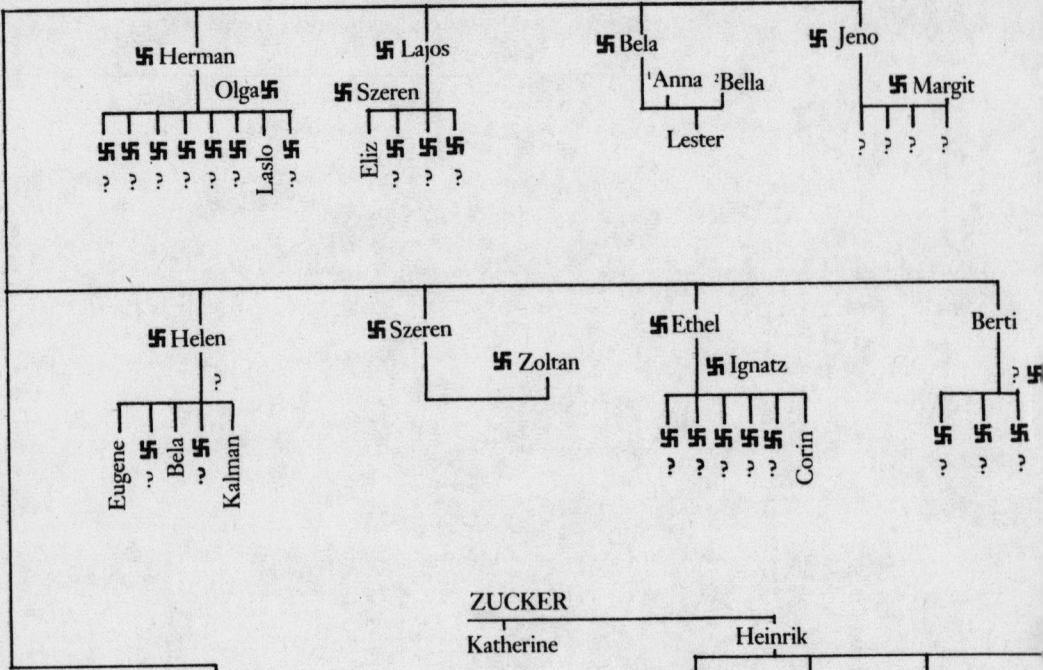
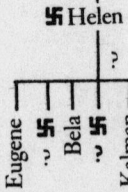
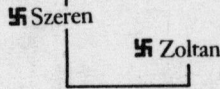
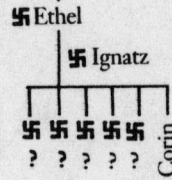
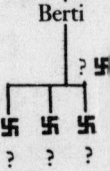
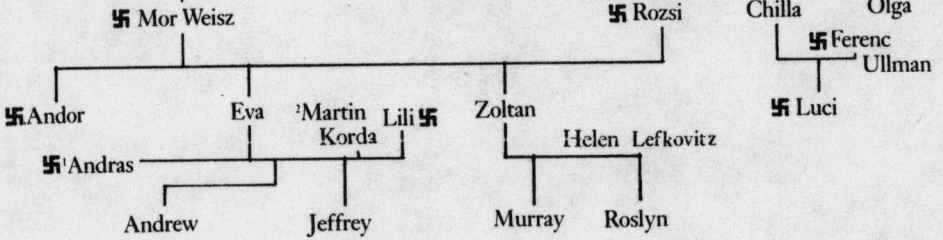